SIMPLE
ACOUSTIC SONGS
THE **EASIEST** EASY GUITAR SONGBOOK EVER

ISBN 978-1-5400-4301-6

HAL•LEONARD®

Visit Hal Leonard Online at
www.halleonard.com

Contact us:
Hal Leonard
7777 West Bluemound Road
Milwaukee, WI 53213
E-mail: info@halleonard.com

In Europe, contact:
Hal Leonard Europe Limited
42 Wigmore Street
Marylebone, London, W1U 2RN
Email: info@halleonardeurope.com

In Australia, contact:
Hal Leonard Australia Pty. Ltd.
4 Lentara Court
Cheltenham, Victoria, 3192 Australia
Email: info@halleonard.com.au

CONTENTS

The A Team

Words and Music by Ed Sheeran

Capo II

Key of A
(Capo Key of G)

G   D/F#   Em7   Cadd9   Am7   C   D5   G5/D

Intro
Fast

Verse

1. White lips, pale face, breath-ing in snow-flakes.
2. Ripped gloves, rain-coat, tried to swim, stay a-float.

Burnt lungs, sour taste.
Dry house, wet clothes.

Light's gone, day's end. Strug-gl-ing to pay rent.
Loose change, bank notes. Wea-ry-eyed, dry throat.

Long nights, strange men.
Call girl, no phone. } And

Pre-Chorus

they say she's in the Class A team. Stuck in her day-

dream. Been this way since eight-een, but late-ly her

face seems slow-ly sink-ing, wast -ing, crum-bl-ing like pas-

- tries. And they scream: The worst things in life come free to us, {1., 2.'cause we're
                                                                      3. and we're

Chorus

*Em7   Cadd9   G

| just   un - der the | up-per hand | and go   mad   for a | cou-ple grams. |

| all   un - der the | up-per hand | and go   mad   for a | cou-ple grams. |

*3rd time, let chords ring (next 12 meas.)

Em7   Cadd9   G

| And she don't wan - na go | out - side | to - night. | And in a |

| And we don't wan - na go | out - side | to - night. | And in a |

Em7   Cadd9   G

| pipe   she flies   to the | Moth-er-land | or sells   love   to an- | oth - er man. ⎱ | |

| pipe   we fly   to the | Moth-er-land | or sell   love   to an- | oth - er man. ⎰ |

3rd time, To Coda ⊕

Em7   Cadd9   G   D5

| It's too cold | out - side | for an | - gels   to |

1.

Em7   Cadd9   G

| fly. | | For an | - gels   to |

Em7   Cadd9   G

| fly. | | | · :‖

2.

Bridge

Am7   Cadd9

| fly.   That | an - gel   will | die | cov-ered   in   white. |

Em7   G

| | Closed   eyes,   an' | hop-in' for a bet-ter life | this |

Am7   Cadd9

| time. | We'll fade out   to | - night | straight down the line. ‖

Interlude   1.

Em7   Cadd9   G

‖: Oo,   oo, | oo. | Oo, | oo.   :‖

2.   ⊕ **Coda**

                         Outro

        D.S. al Coda   w/ Voc. ad lib. on repeats

                                    Em7   Cadd9

| oo.   And | ‖   ‖: fly. | | |

                   1., 2., 3.   4.

G   G5/D   G

| | An - gels   to   :‖ An - gels   to | die. | ‖

Angie

Words and Music by Mick Jagger and Keith Richards

Am E7 Gsus4 Fsus4 F Csus4 C G/B G Dm

Key of Am
Intro
Slow

| Am | | E7 | Gsus4 | Fsus4 F | Csus4 | C | G/B |

let ring

Chorus
Am   Strum   E7   Gsus4   Fsus4 F

1. Angie,   An - gie   when will those clouds all disap -
2. Angie,   you're beautiful,   but ain't   it   time we said good-
3. *Instrumental*

Csus4   C   G/B   Am   E7

pear?   Angie,   An   -   gie,
bye?   Angie,   I   still   love you.

Gsus4   Fsus4   F   Csus4   C

where will   it   lead   us   from   here?   1. With no
Remember   all   those   nights   we   cried.   2. All   the dreams
                                                                            3. Oh,

Verse
G   Dm   Am

lovin'   in our   souls   and   no   money   in   our   coats,
we held   so   close   seemed to   all   go   up   in   smoke.
Angie,   don't   you weep,   oh,   your kiss   - es   still   taste   sweet.

C   F   G   Am

you can't   say   we're satisfied.   But, | Angie,
Let   me   whisper   in your ear,   *(Whispered:)* | *Angie,*
I hate   that   sadness   in your eyes.   But, | Angie,

E7		Gsus4		Fsus4 F		Csus4	C	G/B	1., 2.

An - gie, you can't say we never tried.
Angie, where will it lead us from here?
An - gie, ain't it time we said good -

3.			Interlude						

Csus4   C   G/B   Am   E7   Gsus4   Fsus4 F   Csus4 C

bye?   4. With no

Verse

G   Dm   Am   C   F

lovin' in our souls and no money in our coats, you can't say we're satisfied.

G   Dm   Am

But, Angie, I still love you, ba - by.

Dm   Am   Dm

Everywhere I look, I see your eyes. There ain't a woman that comes

Am   C   F   G

close to you. Come on, baby, dry your eyes.

Outro-Chorus

Am   E7   Gsus4   Fsus4 F   Csus4   C   G/B

Angie, An - gie, ain't it good to be alive?

Am   E7   Gsus4   Fsus4 F   Csus4   C

Angie, An - gie, they can't say we never tried.

Babe, I'm Gonna Leave You

Words and Music by Anne Bredon, Jimmy Page and Robert Plant

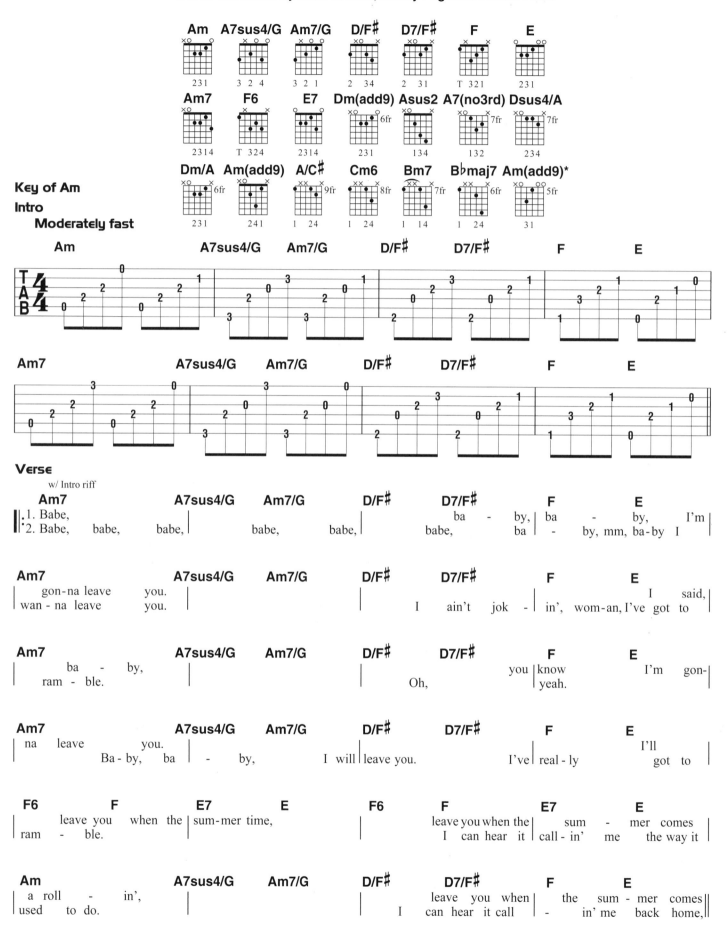

Interlude

Am   Am7   Dm(add9)   Am   Am7   Dm(add9)

etc.

a - long.
whoa.

Am   Am7   Dm(add9)   Am   Am7   Dm(add9)

Bridge

Asus2   A7(no3rd)   Dsus4/A   Dm/A   Am(add9)   A7(no3rd)   Dsus4/A   Dm/A

Play 3 times

```
||----5------------8----||----8----------6----||:----1------------8----||----8----------6----:||
||----------------------||-------7--7------7--||-------------------||-------7--7------7--||
||---4------9-----------||--7----------7------||---4------9--------||--7----------7------||
||-2-----------7--------||--0----------0------||-2-----------7-----||--0----------0------||
||-0-----------0--------||--------------------||-0-----------0-----||--------------------||
||----------------------||--------------------||:------------------||--------------------:||
```

Chorus

Am   Am7/G   D7/F♯   F   E

etc.

|: Ba -   by,   oh,   babe,   I'm gon-na
|: ba -   by,   you know   I've   real - ly

Am   Am7/G   D7/F♯   F   E

| leave   you.   Oh, :||
| got to leave   you.   Oh.

F   E   F   E

I could hear it call - in' me,   I said don't you hear it   call - in' me the way it

Interlude

w/ Interlude pattern

Am   Am7   Dm(add9)   Am   Am7   Dm(add9)

|:* used   to do?   Oh.   :||

*Sung 1st time only.

Guitar Solo

w/ Intro riff

|: Am   A7sus4/G   Am7/G   D/F♯   D7/F♯   F   E   :||

Verse

w/ Intro riff

Am7   A7sus4/G   Am7/G   D/F♯   D7/F♯   F   E

|:   3. I know,   I know,   I know I nev-er, nev-er, nev-er, nev-er, nev-er gon-na
                     4. Oh.   Wom - an.
  go   a - way.   So

Am7   A7sus4/G   Am7/G   D/F♯   D7/F♯   F   E

| leave   you, babe,   but I got-ta | go a way from this place.
  Wom - an.   I know.   I | know.   Feels
  good,   sweet ba - by.   It was real-ly,

| Am7 | | A7sus4/G Am7/G | D/F# D7/F# | F E |

I got-ta quit you, yeah. Oh,

good to have you back a - gain and I know that one day, ba - by, it's gon - na real-ly

real-ly good. You made me hap-py ev'ry sin-gle

| Am7 | | A7sus4/G Am7/G | D/F# D7/F# | F E |

ba - by, ba - by, ba - by, ba - by,

grow, yes, it is. We gon-na go walk-in' through the park ev'ry day.

day, but now I've got to go a -

Chorus
w/ Chorus pattern

| Am | Am7/G | D7/F# | F E |

ba - by, ba - by, ba - by. Oh. Oh.

way. Oh, my babe. Ev'ry day. Oh, oh,

1.2.

| Am | Am7/G | D7/F# | F E |

My, my, my, my, my, my, babe. Don't you hear it call - in' me?

oh. 5. I'm gon-na leave you,

3.

| F E Am | Am7/G | D7/F# | F E |

(Oo.

| Am | Am7/G | D7/F# | F E |

Oo.) Ba - by, ba - by, ba - by.

Outro
Free time

| F | E |

that's when it's call - in' me. *etc.*

| F | E |

I said, that's when it's call - in' me back home.

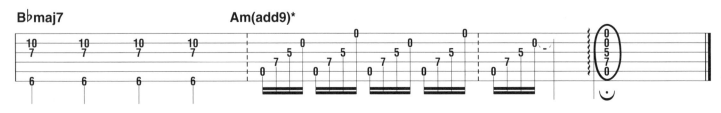

Little Talks

Words and Music by Of Monsters And Men

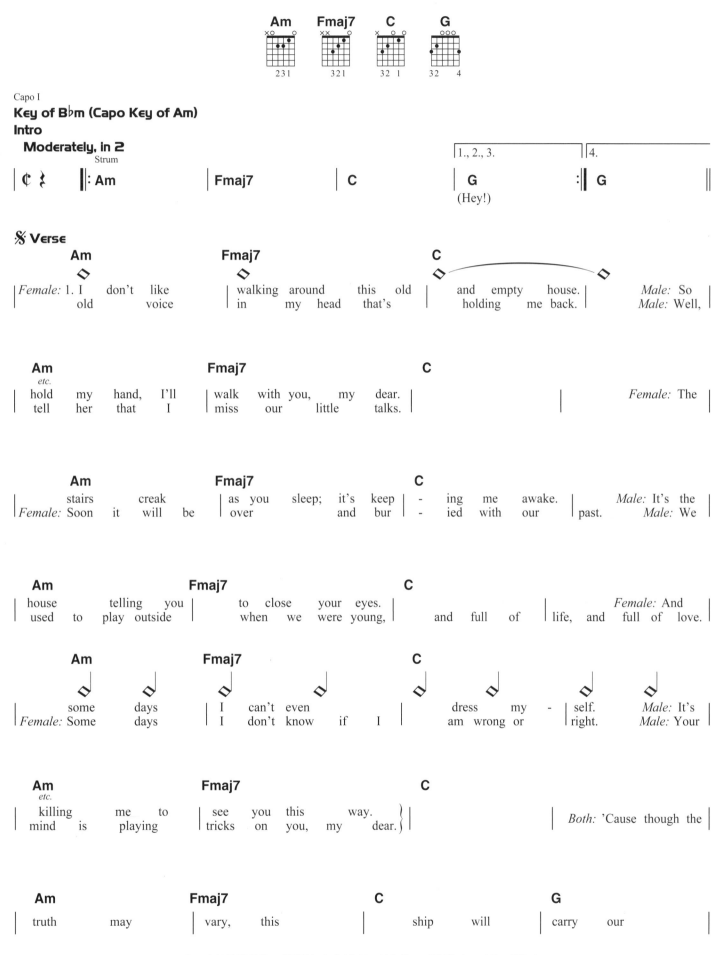

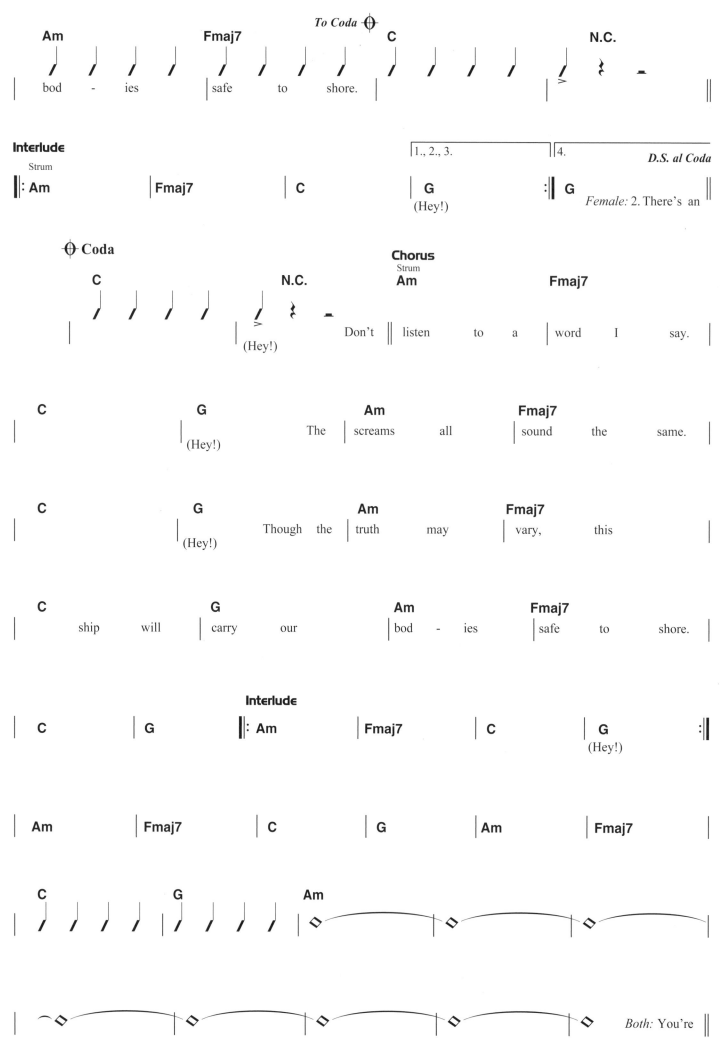

To Coda ⊕

Am / / / /   **Fmaj7** / / / /   **C** / / / /   **N.C.** > 𝄎 ⁃

bod - ies | safe to shore. |

Interlude
Strum

1., 2., 3. ⌐⌐⌐⌐⌐   4.   *D.S. al Coda*

𝄆 **Am** | **Fmaj7** | **C** | **G** 𝄇 **G**
                              (Hey!)   *Female:* 2. There's an

⊕ **Coda**

C / / / /   **N.C.** > 𝄎 ⁃   **Chorus** Strum   **Am**   **Fmaj7**
          (Hey!) Don't ‖ listen to a | word I say. |

C   **G**   **Am**   **Fmaj7**
| | (Hey!) The | screams all | sound the same. |

C   **G**   **Am**   **Fmaj7**
| | (Hey!) Though the | truth may | vary, this |

C   **G**   **Am**   **Fmaj7**
| ship will | carry our | bod - ies | safe to shore. |

Interlude

C | **G**   𝄆 **Am** | **Fmaj7** | **C** | **G** 𝄇
                                                  (Hey!)

Am | **Fmaj7** | **C** | **G** | **Am** | **Fmaj7** |

C / / / /   **G** / / / /   **Am** ◇ ⌒ ◇ ⌒ ◇ ⌒

| ◇ ⌒ | ◇ ⌒ | ◇ ⌒ | ◇ ⌒ | ◇ ⌒ *Both:* You're ‖

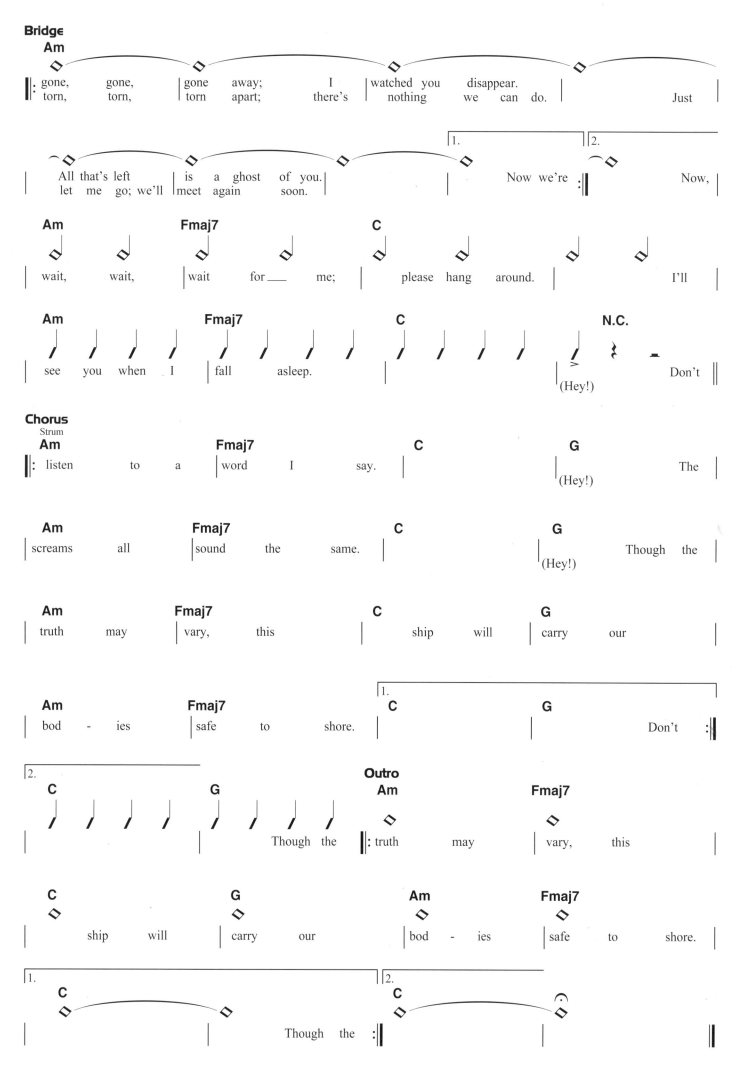

Behind Blue Eyes

Words and Music by Peter Townshend

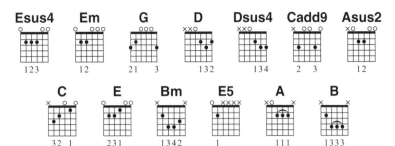

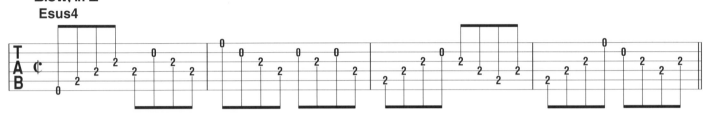

Key of Em
Intro
Slow, in 2

Esus4

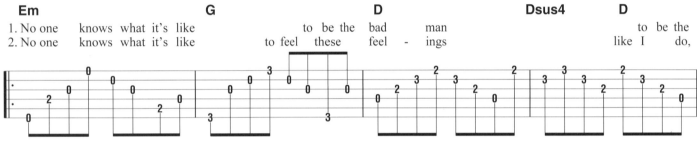

Verse

| Em | G | D | Dsus4 | D |

1. No one   knows what it's like   to be the   bad   man   to be the
2. No one   knows what it's like   to feel these   feel - ings   like I   do,

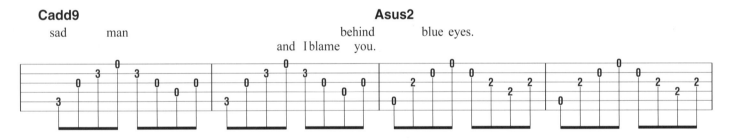

Cadd9   **Asus2**

sad   man   behind   blue eyes.
                                              and I blame   you.

| Em | G | D | Dsus4 | D |

etc.

| No   one   knows what it's like | | to be | hat - ed, | | to be |
| No   one   bites   back as hard | | on their | an - ger; | | none of my |

Cadd9   **Asus2**

| fat - ed | | to telling   on | - ly lies.} | | But   my |
| pain   and woe | | can   show | through. | |

Chorus

| C | D | G | C | D |
Strum
| dreams | | they aren't as | empty | | as my | con - science | seems   to be. |

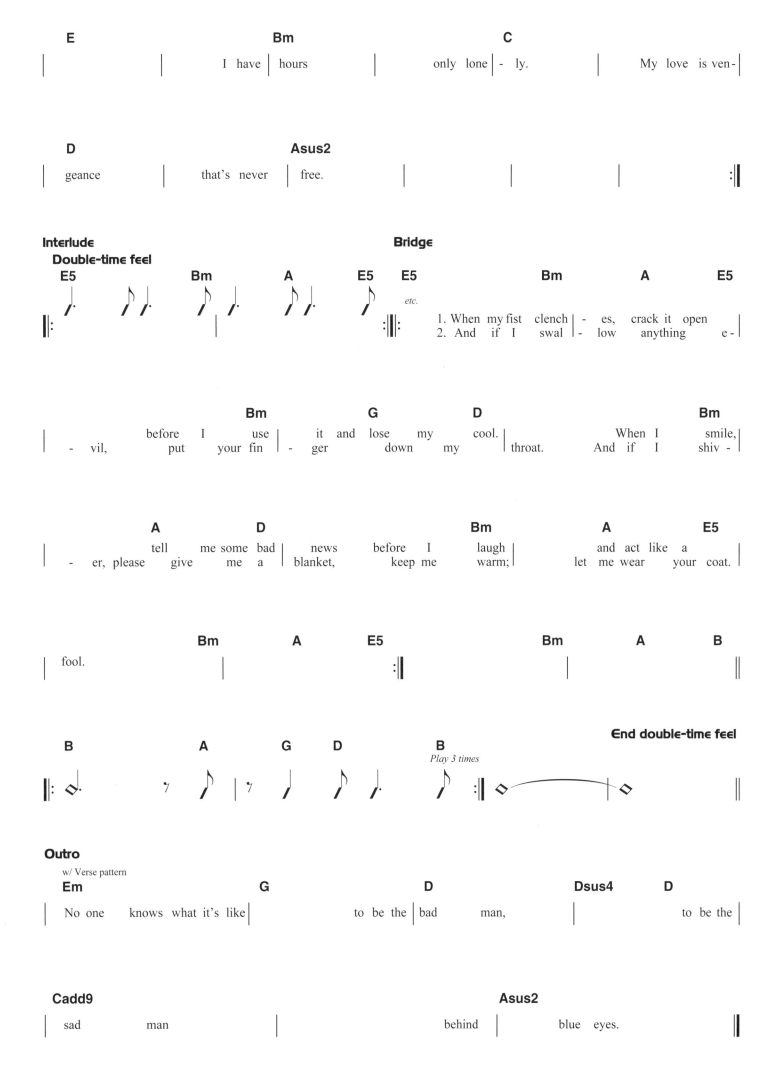

Blowin' in the Wind

Words and Music by Bob Dylan

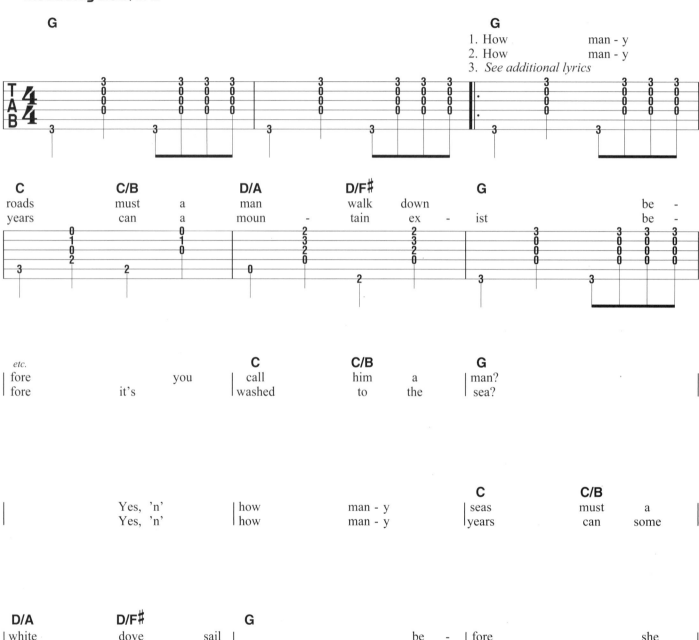

Capo VII

Key of D (Capo Key of G)

Intro

Moderately slow, in 2

Verse

1. How man - y
2. How man - y
3. *See additional lyrics*

roads must a man walk down be -
years can a moun - tain ex - ist be -

etc.
fore you call him a man?
fore it's washed to the sea?

Yes, 'n' how man - y seas must a
Yes, 'n' how man - y years can some

white dove sail be - fore she
peo - ple ex - ist be - fore they're al -

sleeps in the sand?
lowed to be free?

Yes, 'n'
Yes, 'n'

G			C	C/B		D/A		D/F♯	
how	man - y		times	must the		can - non - balls		fly	
how	man - y		times	can a		man	turn	his	

G							C	C/B	
head,		be -	fore	they're		for -	ev -	er	
head,		pre -	tend - . ing	he		just	does -	n't	

G					C	C/B	
banned?			The		an -	swer,	my
see?							

D/A		D/F♯		G			C	C/G	
friend,		is		blow - in' in	the		wind.	The	

C		C/B		D/A		D/F♯		G	
an -		swer is		blow - in'	in	the wind.			

Harmonica Solo

C	C/B		D/A	D/F♯		G	

C	C/G		C	C/B		D/A	D/F♯

		1.2.		3.
G				

Additional Lyrics

3. How many times must a man look up before he can see the sky?
   Yes, 'n' how many ears must one man have before he can hear people cry?
   Yes, 'n' how many deaths will it take till he knows that too many people have died?
   The answer, my friend, is blowin' in the wind.
   The answer is blowin' in the wind.

Broken Halos

Words and Music by Chris Stapleton and Mike Henderson

G5   Csus2   Em7   Bm   Gsus4   G   C   G/B   G5/A

Capo I

Key of A♭ (Capo Key of G)

Chorus

Moderately

Strum

G5 ... **Csus2** **G5** ... **Em7** **G5**

$\frac{4}{4}$ Seen my share of | broken halos, | folded wings that |

Csus2 **G5** ... **Csus2** **G5**

| used to fly. | They've all gone | wherever they go, |

2nd time, To Coda 1 ⊕

3rd time, To Coda 2 ⊕

Em7 **G5** **Csus2** **G5** ... **Em7** **G5** ... **Csus2** **G5**

| broken halos that | used to shine. | | ‖

Verse

G5 ... **Csus2** **G5** ... **Em7** **G5** ... **Csus2** **G5**

| 1. Angels come down | from the heaven | just to help us | on our way. |

D.C. al Coda 1

Csus2 **G5** ... **Em7** **G5** ... **Csus2** **G5**

| Come to teach us, | then they leave us, | and they find some other | soul to save. ‖

Coda 1

Csus2	G5		Em7	G5		Csus2	G5

| used to shine, | | broken halos that | used to shine. ‖

Interlude

| Bm | | G | Gsus4 G | Bm | |

| C | | | | | |

Verse

| G5 | | Csus2 | G5 |
‖ 2. Don't go lookin' | for the reasons. |

| Em7 | G5 | | Csus2 | G5 | | | Csus2 | G5 |
| Don't go askin' | Jesus why. | We're not meant to | know the answers. |

D.C. al Coda 2

| Em7 | G5 | | Csus2 | G5 | | Em7 | G5 | | Csus2 | G5 |
| They belong to the | by and by. | They belong to the by | and by. ‖

Coda 2

| Csus2 | G5 | | Em7 | G5 | | Csus2 | G5 |
| used to shine, | | broken halos that | used to shine, |

| Em7 | G5 | | Csus2 | G5 | | Em7 | G5 | | Csus2 G/B G5/A G5 |
| broken halos that | used to shine, | | broken halos that | used to shine. ‖

Can't Find My Way Home

Words and Music by Steve Winwood

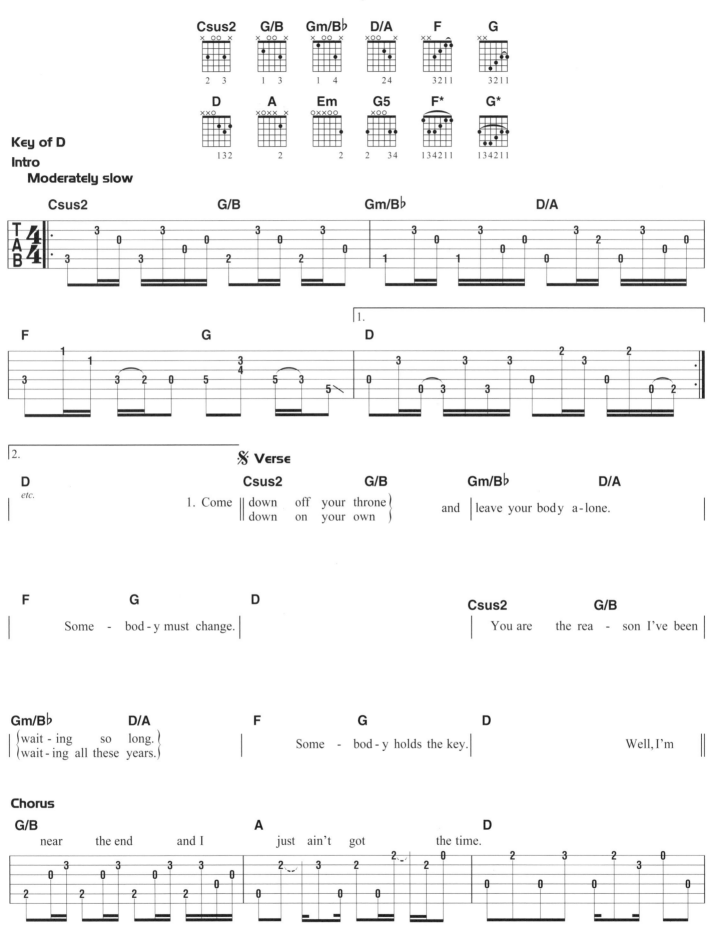

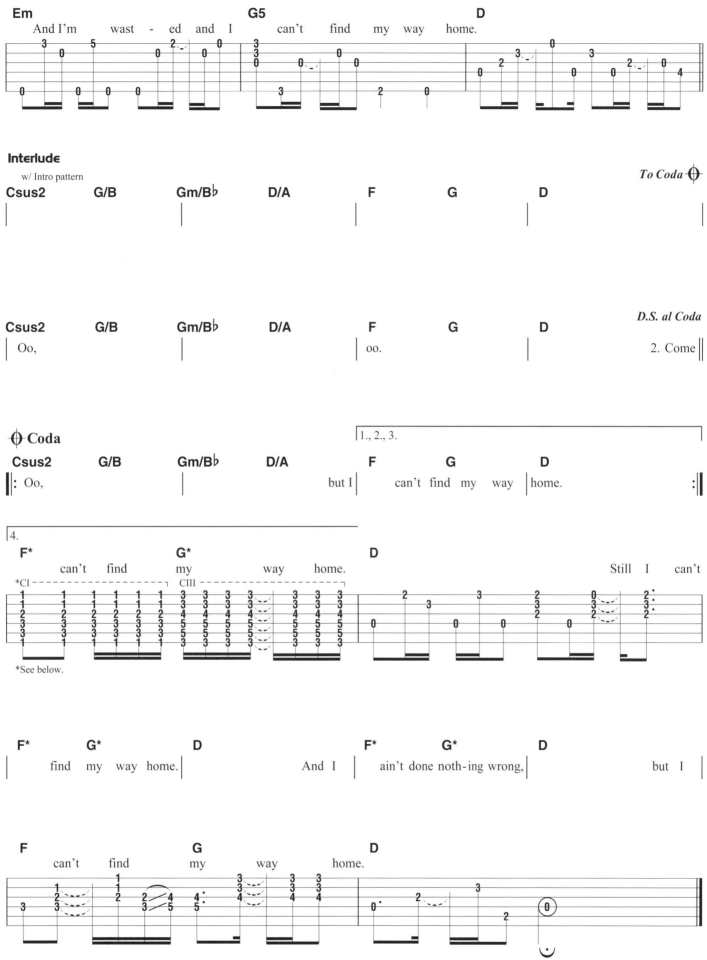

*"C" denotes barre. Fractional prefix indicates which strings are barred (e.g. 1/2 = first 3 strings).
 Roman numeral suffix indicates barred fret.

Change the World

featured on the Motion Picture Soundtrack PHENOMENON

Words and Music by Wayne Kirkpatrick, Gordon Kennedy and Tommy Sims

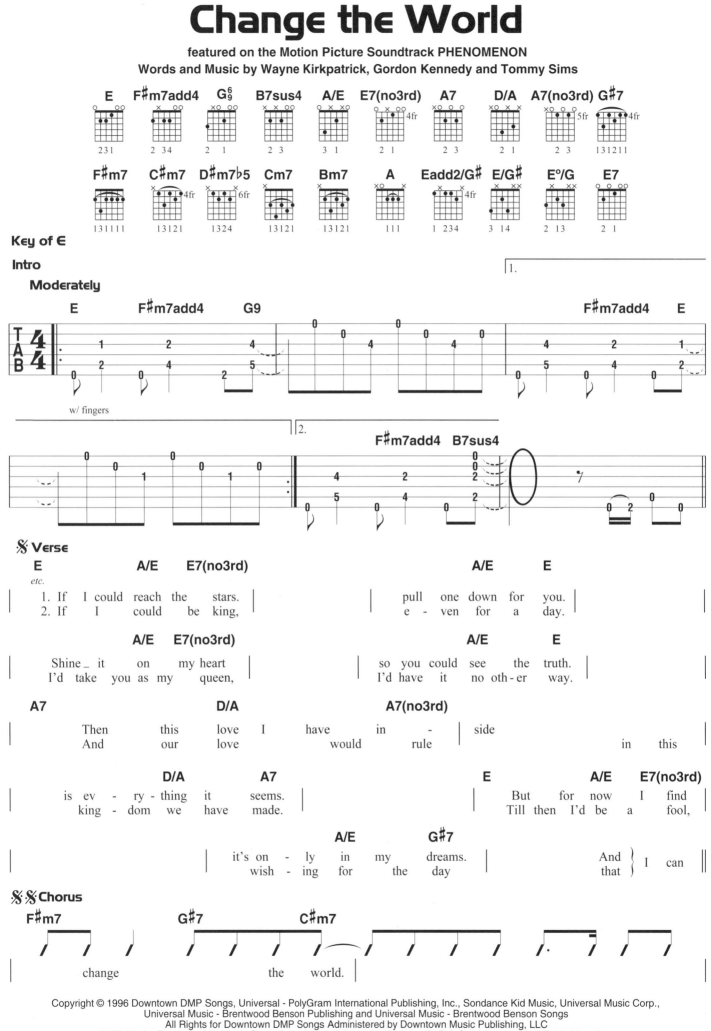

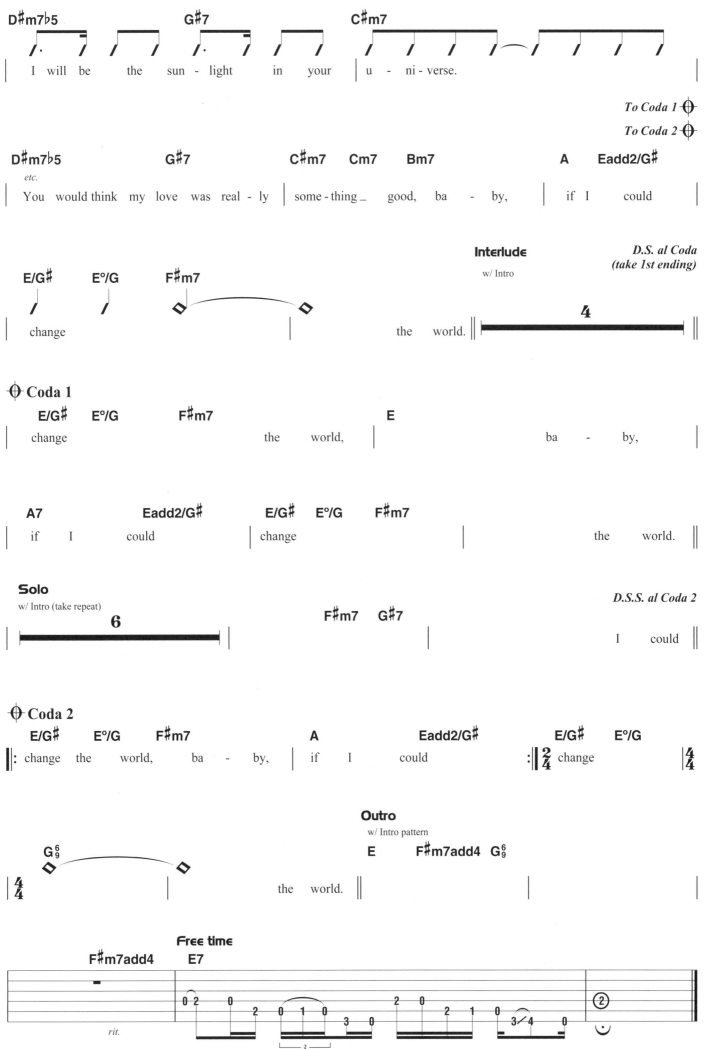

D#m7b5   **G#7**   **C#m7**

I will be the sun - light in your | u - ni - verse.

To Coda 1 ⊕
To Coda 2 ⊕

D#m7b5   **G#7**   **C#m7** **Cm7** **Bm7**   **A** **Eadd2/G#**
etc.

You would think my love was real - ly | some-thing _ good, ba - by, | if I could |

E/G# **E°/G** **F#m7**

Interlude   *D.S. al Coda*
w/ Intro   *(take 1st ending)*

change | | the world. ‖ ____4____ ‖

⊕ **Coda 1**

E/G# **E°/G** **F#m7**   **E**

change the world, | ba - by, |

A7   **Eadd2/G#** **E/G#** **E°/G** **F#m7**

if I could | change | the world. ‖

Solo
w/ Intro (take repeat)   *D.S.S. al Coda 2*

____6____   **F#m7** **G#7**   I could ‖

⊕ **Coda 2**

E/G# **E°/G** **F#m7**   **A**   **Eadd2/G#**   **E/G#** **E°/G**

‖: change the world, ba - by, | if I could :‖ **2/4** change | **4/4**

Outro
w/ Intro pattern

G6/9   **E** **F#m7add4** **G6/9**

4/4 | | the world. ‖ | |

Free time

F#m7add4 **E7**

rit.

23

Daughter

Words by Eddie Vedder
Music by Eddie Vedder, Stone Gossard, Jeff Ament, Mike McCready and Dave Abbruzzese

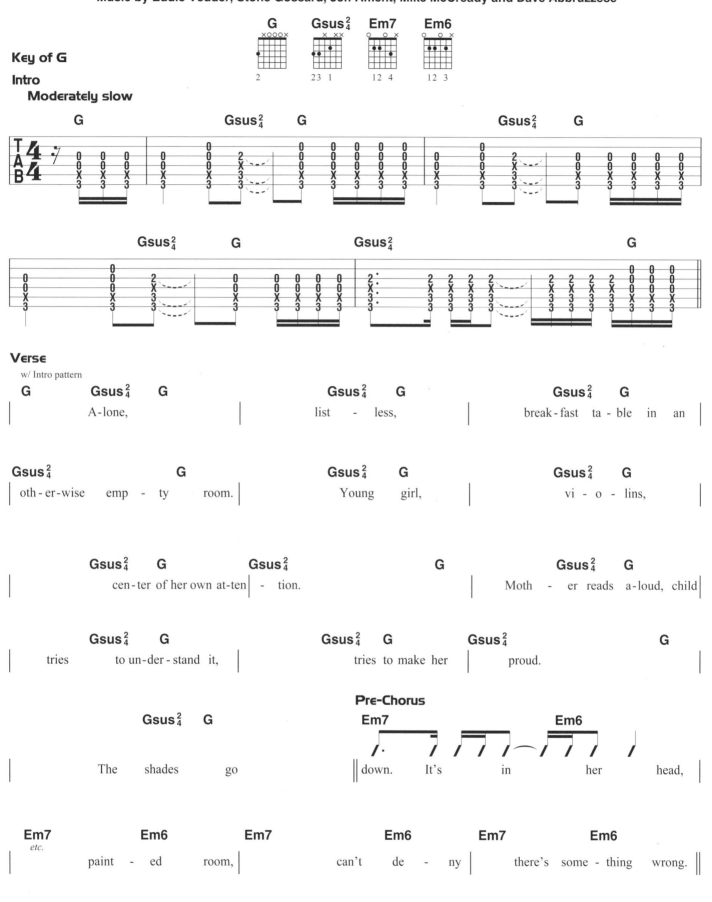

𝄋 Chorus

w/ Intro pattern

G	Gsus²₄	G	Gsus²₄	G	Gsus²₄	G
me.}	Don't call	me daught er,	not fit	to.	The pic - ture kept	

Gsus²₄	G	Gsus²₄	G	Gsus²₄	G
will re - mind	me. Don't call	me daugh-ter,	not fit	to. / to be. }	

To Coda ⊕

Gsus²₄	G	Gsus²₄	G	Gsus²₄	G
The pic - ture kept	will re - mind	me. Don't call	me...		

Interlude

w/ Pre-Chorus pattern

Em7	Em6	G	Gsus²₄
		Play 4 times	

Bridge

Em7	Em6	Em7
	She holds	the hand

Em6	Em7	Em6	Em7
etc. that holds	her down.	She will	rise a - bove.

Guitar Solo

w/ Intro pattern

G	Gsus²₄	G	Gsus²₄	G	Gsus²₄	G

Gsus²₄	G	G

Chorus

Gsus²₄	G
Don't call me daugh-ter,	not fit to.

Gsus²₄	G	Gsus²₄	G
etc. The pic - ture kept	will re - mind	me. Don't call	me daugh-ter,

D.S. al Coda

Gsus²₄	G	Gsus²₄	G
not fit to be.	The pic - ture kept	will re - mind	

⊕ Coda

Interlude

w/ Pre-Chorus pattern

Outro

w/ Lead Voc. ad lib. on repeats

Repeat and fade

Em7	Em6	Em7
Play 8 times		The shades go down.

2 3 2 2 3 2 2 3 2 2 3 2 2 3 2 2 3 2 2 3 2 2 3 2 2 3 2 2 3 2 2 3 2 2 3 2

Dear Prudence

Words and Music by John Lennon and Paul McCartney

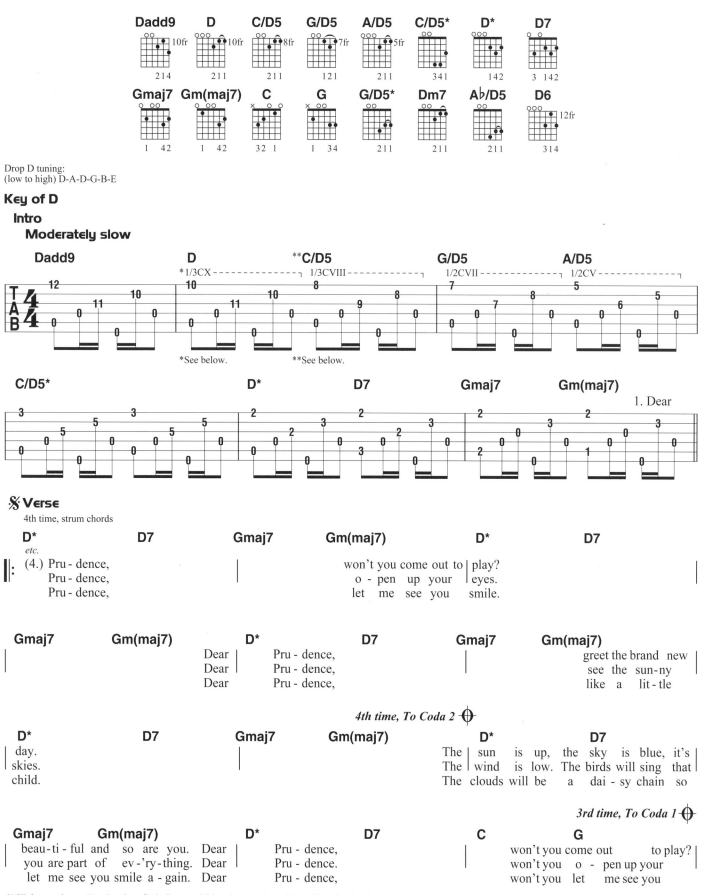

Drop D tuning:
(low to high) D-A-D-G-B-E

Key of D

Intro

Moderately slow

*See below. **See below.

1. Dear

§ **Verse**

4th time, strum chords

etc.

(4.) Pru - dence,	won't you come out to	play?
Pru - dence,	o - pen up your	eyes.
Pru - dence,	let me see you	smile.

Dear	Pru - dence,	greet the brand new
Dear	Pru - dence,	see the sun-ny
Dear	Pru - dence,	like a lit - tle

4th time, To Coda 2 ⊕

day.	The	sun is up, the sky is blue, it's
skies.	The	wind is low. The birds will sing that
child.		The clouds will be a dai - sy chain so

3rd time, To Coda 1 ⊕

beau - ti - ful and so are you. Dear	Pru - dence,	won't you come out to play?
you are part of ev - 'ry-thing. Dear	Pru - dence.	won't you o - pen up your
let me see you smile a - gain. Dear	Pru - dence,	won't you let me see you

*"C" denotes barre. Fractional prefix indicates which strings are barred (e.g. 1/2 = first 3 strings).
Roman numeral suffix indicates barred fret.

In this arrangement, chord symbols ending in /D5 denote **polychords: two distinct chords played together, one above the other.

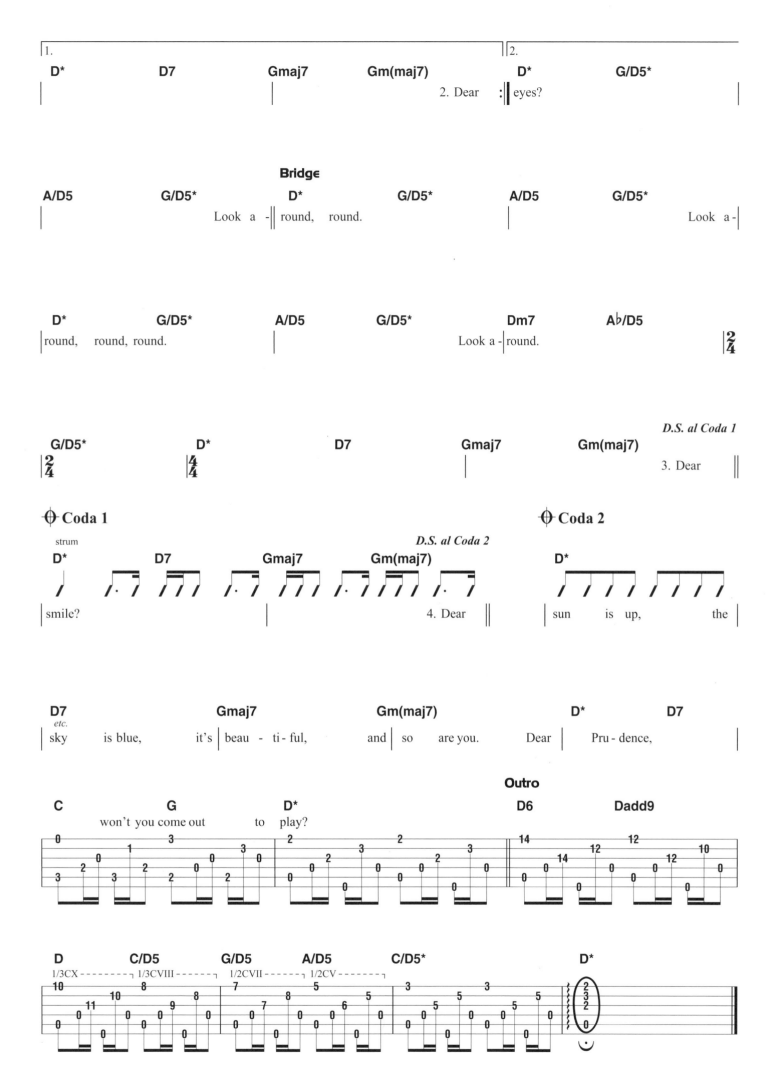

Drops of Jupiter
(Tell Me)

Words and Music by Pat Monahan, Jimmy Stafford, Rob Hotchkiss, Charlie Colin and Scott Underwood

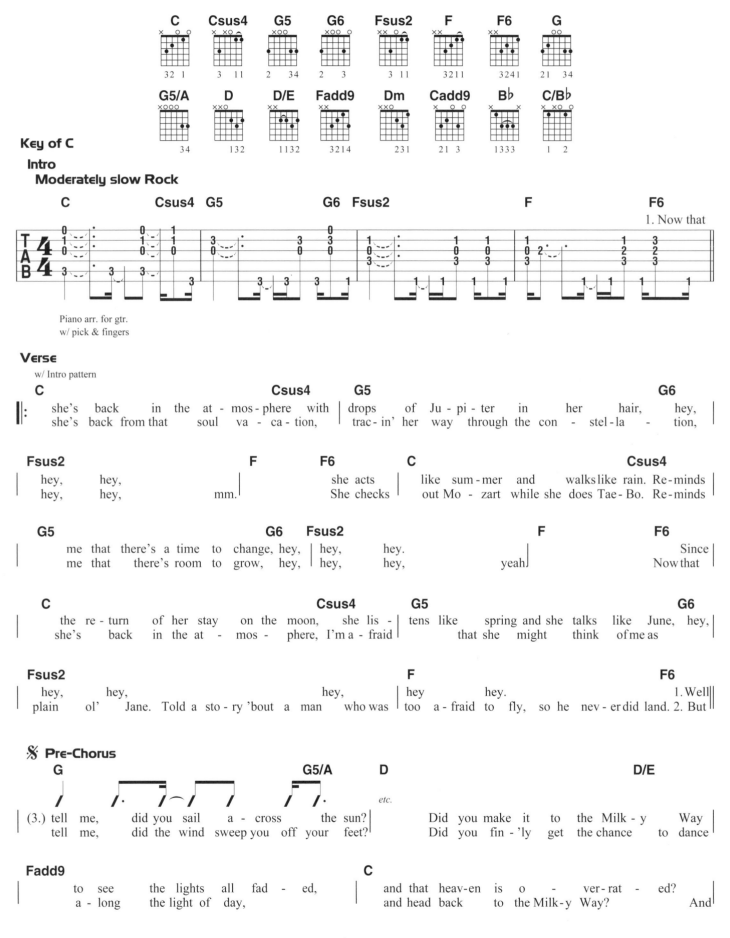

G   **G5/A**   **D**

| Tell me, | did you fall | from a shoot-ing star, | | one | with-out a per-ma-nent |
| tell me, | did Ve-nus | blow your | mind? Was it ev-'ry-thing you want-ed to find? |

Dm ◇   **Fadd9** ◇

scar, } and did   you miss me while you were   look-in' for { 1., 2. your-self   out   there?
                                                          { 3. your-self?

1.

Interlude

w/ Intro pattern

C   **Csus4**   **G5**   **G6** **Fsus2**   **F**   **F6**

                                                                                            2. Now that :‖

2.

Chorus

Cadd9   **G6**

* (Na,   na,   na,   na,   na,   na, | na   na,   na,   na,   na,   na,

*Bkgd. voc. sung 2nd & 3rd times only.

Fsus2

                         2. And did you fin-'ly get the chance to dance | a - long   the light of day?

na,   na.

Cadd9   **G6**

love,   pride,   deep - fried chick-en,   your | best   friend   al - ways   stick-in'
                                                  And did   you
Na,   na,   na,   na,   na,   na,   na,   na,   na,   na,   na,   na,

Fsus2

up   for   you   e - ven when I know you're   wrong? Can you im-ag-ine no
fall   from a shoot-ing star,   fall   from a shoot-ing   star?
na,   na.

Cadd9   **G6**

first   dance,   freeze - dried ro - mance, | five   hour   phone con - ver-sa - tion, the
                                                  And are   you
Na,   na,   na,   na,   na,   na,   na,   na,   na,   na,   na,   na,

                                                                                            Fine

B♭   **C/B♭**   **B♭**   **F** ◇

best   soy   lat - te that you ev - er had   and | me?   But ‖
lone - ly look-in' for   your - self out   there?
na,   na.)

Pre-Chorus

G   **G5/A**   **D**   **D/E**

tell me,   did the wind sweep you   off your feet?   Did you fin-'ly   get the chance   to dance

                                                                           D.S. al Fine
                                                              (take 2nd ending)

Fadd9   **C**

          a - long   the light of day,   and head   back   to the Milk - y Way?   And ‖

Give a Little Bit

Words and Music by Rick Davies and Roger Hodgson

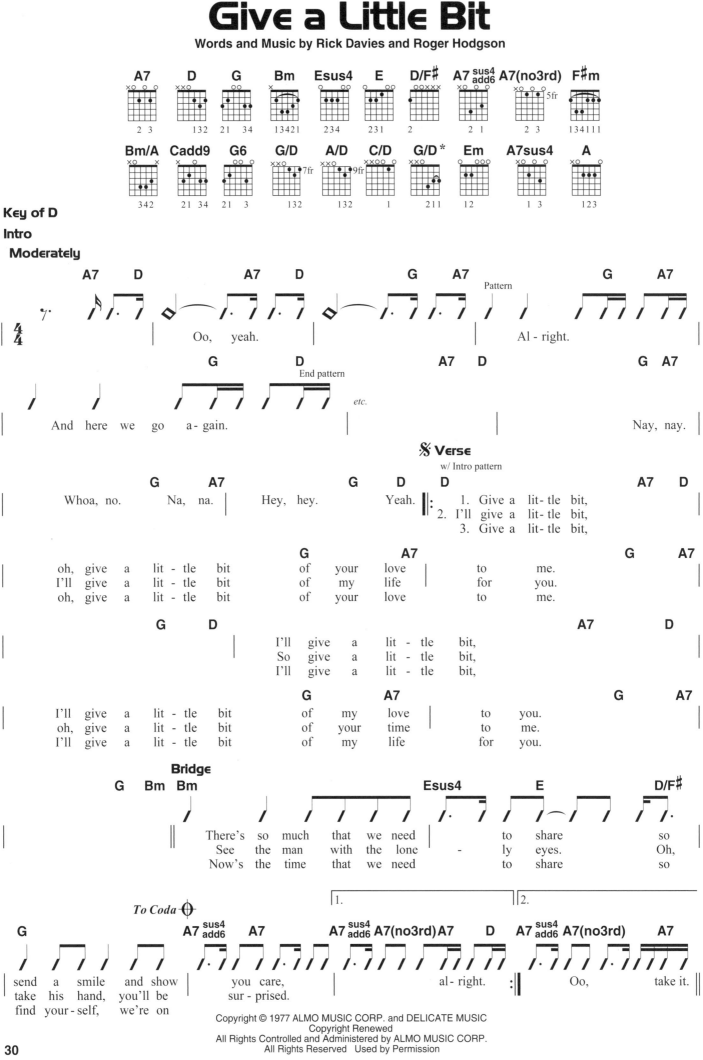

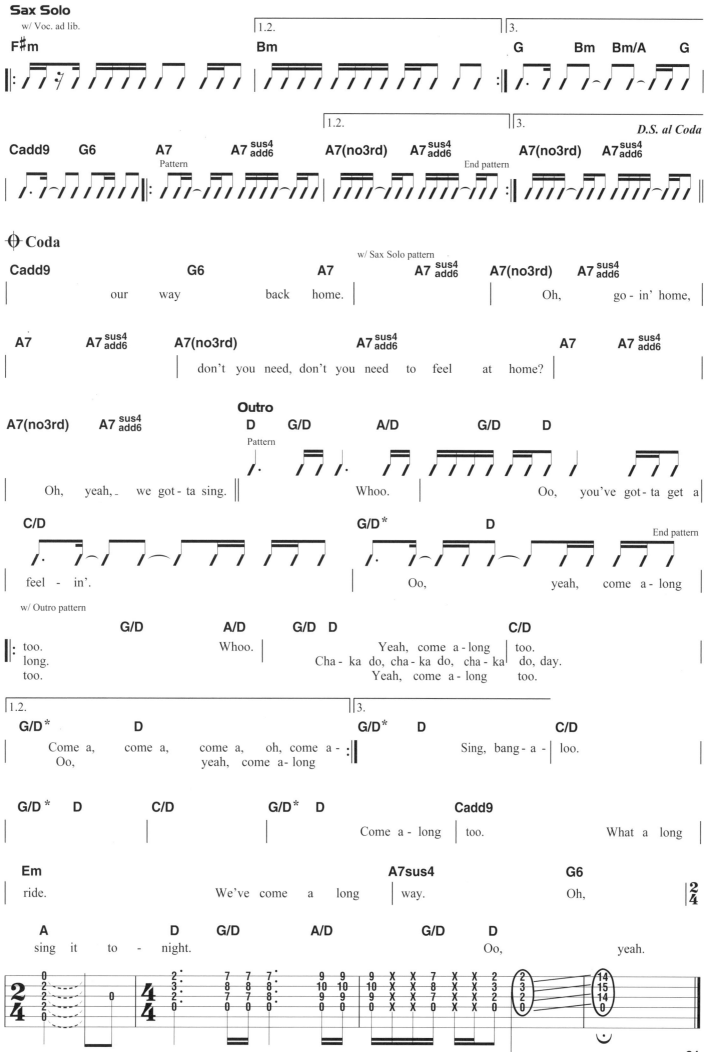

Half of My Heart

Words and Music by John Mayer

Chord diagrams: B♭ (1333), F (3211), C (32 1), Dm7 (211), Am7 (2 1), Cm7 (13121), Gm7 (131111)

Key of F

Intro

Moderately

Verse

B♭ F C Dm7 B♭ F C

etc.
1. I was born in the arms of i-mag-i-nar-y friends;
2. I was made to be-lieve I'd nev-er love some-bod-y else.

B♭ F C Dm7 B♭ F C

free to roam, made a home out of ev-'ry-where I've been.   Then
Made a plan, stay the man who can on-ly love him - self.   Lone-

B♭ F C Dm7

you come crash-ing in like a real - est thing.   Try 'n'
- ly was the song I sang till the day you came,   and show-

B♭ F C

my best to un-der-stand all that your love can bring. }   Oh,
- ing me an-oth-er way, and all that my love can bring. }

Chorus

B♭ F C Dm7 B♭ F C

half of my heart's got a grip on the sit-u-a-tion, half of my heart takes time.

B♭ F C Dm7 B♭

Half of my heart's got a right mind to tell you that I can't keep lov-ing you, (Can't keep lov-ing you.)

| C   F   C | 1. Dm7   Bb   F   C |
| oh, with half of my heart. | | | | |

| 2.
| Dm7   Bb   Dm7   Bb | F   C   Dm7   Bb |
| :‖   With half of my heart. | | | Your faith ‖

Bridge

| F   Am7   Cm7   Gm7 |
| is strong, | but I can | on - ly fall short for so | long.   Down the road, |

| F   Am7   Cm7   Gm7 |
| lat - er on, | you will | hate that I nev - er gave | more   to you   than |

| Bb   C |
| half of my heart, | but I | can't stop lov-ing you. (I | can't stop   lov-ing you.) I |

| Bb   C   N.C. |
| can't stop   lov-ing you. (I | can't stop   lov-ing you.) I | can't stop   lov-ing you | with half of my, |

| Bb   F   C   Dm7   Bb   F   C |
| half of my heart, | oh, | half of my heart. | ‖

Outro-Chorus

| Bb   F   C   Dm7   Bb   F   C |
‖: Half of my heart's got a real	good i - mag-i-na tion,	half of my heart's got you.
‖: Half of my heart is a shot	- gun wed-ding to a bride	with a pa-per ring.	And
Half of my heart,	oh,	half of my heart.

Play 3 times and fade

| Bb   F   C   Dm7   Bb   F   C |
| Half of my heart's got a right| mind to tell you that | half of my heart won't do. |
| half of my heart is the part | of a man who's nev-er | tru - ly loved an - y-thing. |
| Half of my heart, | oh, | half of my heart.   :‖

33

Hey You

Words and Music by Roger Waters

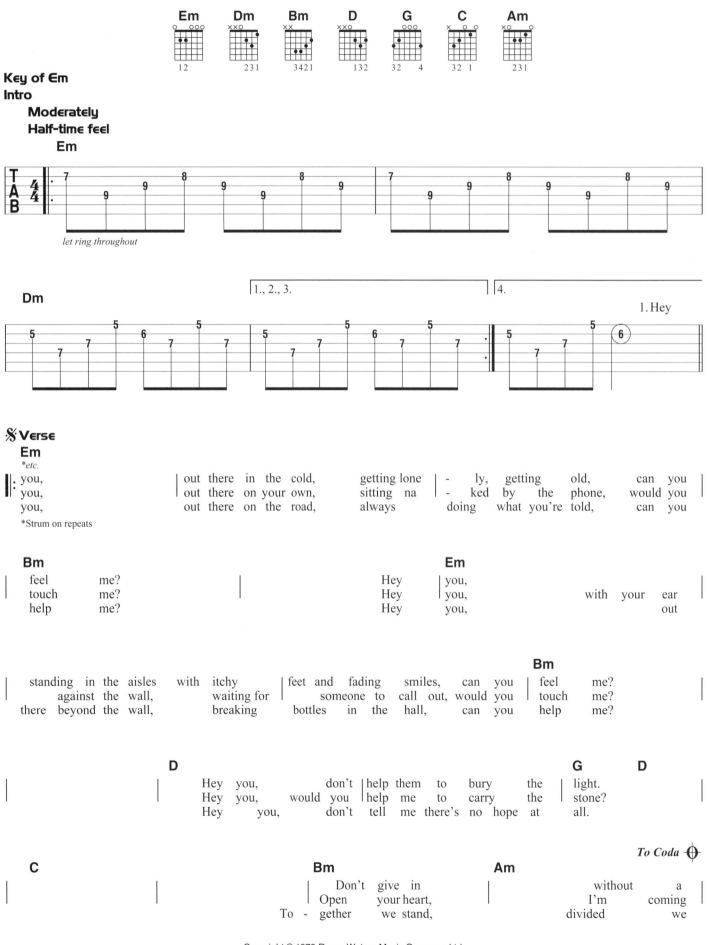

Key of Em
Intro
Moderately
Half-time feel

%Verse

*etc.

you,	out there in the cold,	getting lone	- ly, getting old,	can you
you,	out there on your own,	sitting na	- ked by the phone,	would you
you,	out there on the road,	always	doing what you're told,	can you

*Strum on repeats

feel	me?		Hey	you,	
touch	me?		Hey	you,	with your ear
help	me?		Hey	you,	out

standing in the aisles	with itchy	feet and fading smiles, can you	feel	me?
against the wall,	waiting for	someone to call out, would you	touch	me?
there beyond the wall,	breaking	bottles in the hall, can you	help	me?

Hey you,	don't	help them to bury the	light.
Hey you,	would you	help me to carry the	stone?
Hey you,	don't	tell me there's no hope at	all.

To Coda

Don't give in	without a
Open your heart,	I'm coming
To - gether we stand,	divided we

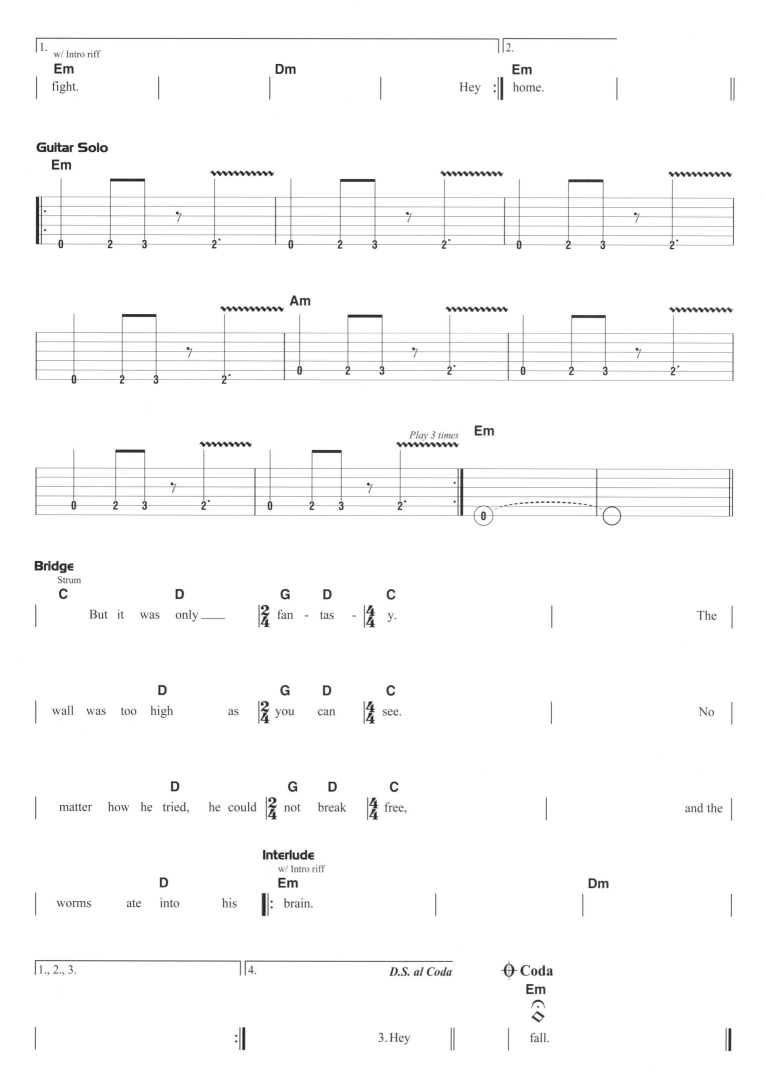

Home

Words and Music by Greg Holden and Drew Pearson

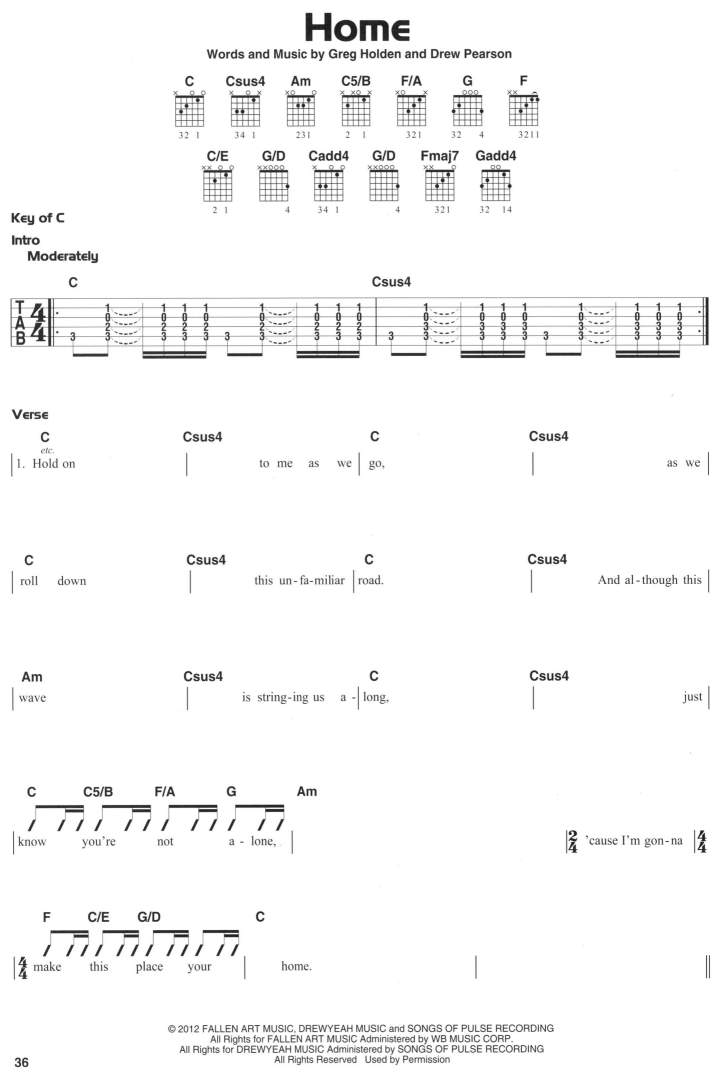

% Verse

| C | Cadd4 | C | Cadd4 |

2., 3. Set-tle down,   it-'ll all   be | clear.

| C | Cadd4 | C | Cadd4 |

Don't pay no mind to the | de-mons; they fill you with | fear.

| Am | F | C | G |

Trou-ble, it might drag you | down.   You get | lost, you can al-ways be | found.   Just |

| C | C5/B | F/A | G | Am |

know   you're   not   a - lone, | $\frac{2}{4}$ 'cause I'm gon-na $\frac{4}{4}$

| F | C/E | G/D | C |

$\frac{4}{4}$ make   this   place   your | home.

Interlude

| *Fmaj7 | C | Am |

1. Oo,   oo.
2. - 6. Oh,   oh.

*6th time, let chords ring.

6th time, To Coda ⊕

| Gadd4 | Fmaj7 | C |

Oo.
Oh.

| Gadd4 |

| 1.2. | 3. | *D.S. al Coda* (take repeats) | ⊕ **Coda** |

G 🠗

House of Gold

Words and Music by Tyler Joseph

C   F   Am   G   A   Dm   B♭m

Key of C
Intro
Moderately
N.C.(C)

TAB 4/4

Ukulele arr. for gtr., next 12 meas.

She

Chorus
w/ Intro riff
N.C.(C)

| asked me, "Son, when | I grow old, will | you buy me a | house of gold? And |

| when your father | turns to stone, will | you take care of | me?" She ‖

Chorus
Strum

| C | | F | | Am | | G |
‖: asked me, "Son, when | I grow old, will | you buy me a | house of gold? And |

| C | | F | | C G | C |
| when your father | turns to stone, will | you take care of | me?" ‖

Bridge

| F | | A | | Dm | | B♭m |
| I will | make you | queen of | everything you |

| **F**
| see.   I'll put you on the map, | **C**   I'll cure you of disease. | **F** | **C** | {1. Let's ‖
{2. And ‖

Verse

| **C**
| say   we   up   and | **F** left   this   town   and | **Am** turned   our   future |
| since   we   know   that | dreams   are   dead   and   and | life   turns   plans   up |

| **G**
| upside   down.   We'll | **C** make   pretend   that | **F** you   and   me   lived | **C**   **G** ever   after |
| on   their   head.   I | will   plan   to | be   a   bum   so | I   just   might   be - |

| 1.
| **C**
| happily. | | She | :‖ come   someone! | | She ‖

| 2.
| **C**

Chorus

| **C**
| asked   me, "Son, when | **F** I   grow   old,   will | **Am** you   buy   me   a | **G** house   of   gold?   And |

| **C**
| when   your   father | **F** turns   to   stone,   will | **C** you   take   care | **G** of | **C** me?" ‖

Outro

| **F** ◇
| I   will | **A** ◇ make   you | **Dm** ◇ queen   of | **B♭m** ◇ everything   you |

| **F** ◇
| see.   I'll put you on   the map, | **C** ◇ I'll cure you of   disease. | **F** ◇ ‖

I Got a Name

Words by Norman Gimbel
Music by Charles Fox

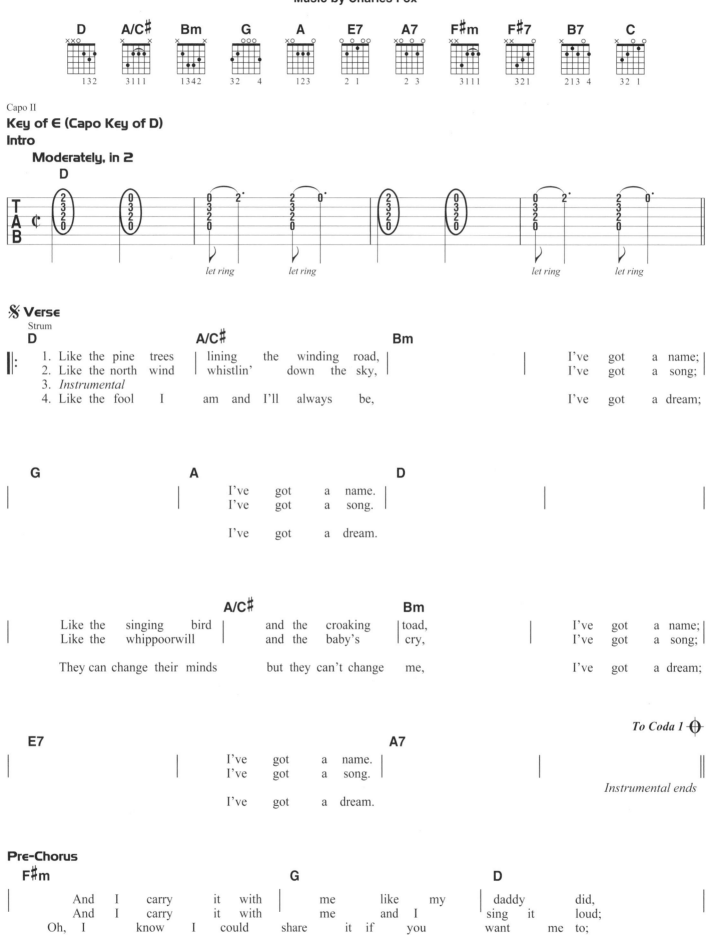

Capo II

Key of E (Capo Key of D)
Intro

Moderately, in 2

𝄋 **Verse**

Strum

D   **A/C♯**   **Bm**

1. Like the pine trees | lining the winding road, | | I've got a name;
2. Like the north wind | whistlin' down the sky, | | I've got a song;
3. *Instrumental*
4. Like the fool I am and I'll always be, | | I've got a dream;

G   **A**   **D**

I've got a name.
I've got a song.

I've got a dream.

              A/C♯   **Bm**

Like the singing bird | and the croaking |toad, | I've got a name;
Like the whippoorwill | and the baby's |cry, | I've got a song;

They can change their minds | but they can't change me, | | I've got a dream;

To Coda 1 ⊕

E7   **A7**

I've got a name.
I've got a song.

I've got a dream.

Instrumental ends

Pre-Chorus
F♯m   **G**   **D**

And I carry it with | me like my | daddy did,
And I carry it with | me and I | sing it loud;
Oh, I know I could share it if you | want me to;

F#7
but I'm living the dream | that he kept
if it gets me no - where, | I'll go there
if you're goin' my way, | I'll go with

Bm   **E7**

Chorus

A7   **F#m**   **G**
hid.
proud. | Movin' me down the high | - way,
you.

F#m   **B7**   **G**   **A**
rollin' me down the high | - way, | movin' ahead so life | won't pass me by.

To Coda 2 ⊕ | 1. | 2.   *D.S. al Coda 1*

C

⊕ **Coda 1**   *D.S. al Coda 2*

D
And I'm gonna go | there free.

⊕ **Coda 2**

         F#m   **G**   **F#m**
Movin' me down the high | - way, | rollin' me down the high -

B7   **G**   **A**
- way, | movin' ahead so life | won't pass me by.

C   **D**

If I Had $1,000,000

Words and Music by Steven Page and Ed Robertson

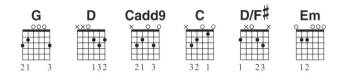

Capo II

Key of A (Capo Key of G)

Intro

Moderately, in 2

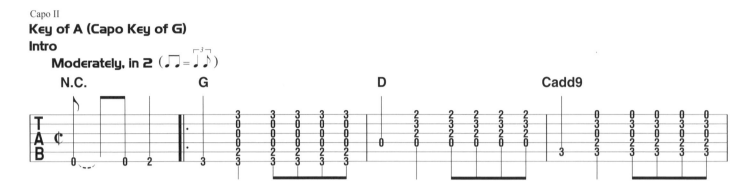

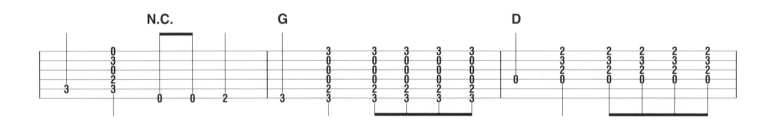

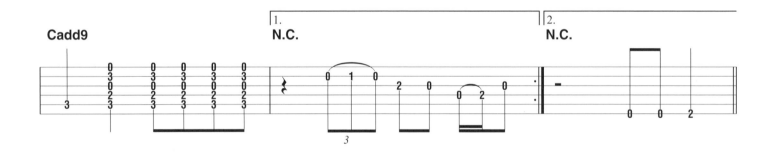

Verse

Strum

G		D		C			
1. If I	had a	million	dol - lars,	(If I	had a	million	dol -
2. If I	had a	million	dol - lars,	(If I	had a	million	dol -
3. If I	had a	million	dol - lars,	(If I	had a	million	dol -

G		D		C			
- lars)	well, I'd	buy you a	house.		(I would buy	you	a house.)
- lars)	well, I'd	buy you a	fur coat.		(But not a	real fur coat,	that's cruel.)
- lars)	well, I'd	buy you a	green dress.		(But not a	real green dress,	that's cruel.)

G		**D**		**C**	

```
G                    D                              C
|                And if  I  | had  a  million  dol |- lars,   (If  I  | had  a  million  dol -|
                 And if  I  | had  a  million  dol |- lars,   (If  I  | had  a  million  dol -|
                 And if  I    had  a  million  dol  - lars,   (If  I    had  a  million  dol -

G                    D                              C
| - lars)  I'd buy  you  | furniture   for your house.|        (Maybe   a  nice | Chesterfield ___ or  an ot-|
  - lars)  well, I'd buy  | you an  exotic      pet.  |        (Yep,  like  a   | llama,           or  an e-|
  - lars)      well, I'd    buy       you some  art.           (A  Pi - casso,     or ___ a  Gar -

G                    D                              C
| toman.)  And if  I  | had  a  million  dol |- lars,   (If  I  | had  a  million  dol -|
  mu.)     And if  I  | had  a  million  dol |- lars,   (If  I  | had  a  million  dol -|
  funkel.) And if  I    had  a  million  dol  - lars,   (If  I    had  a  million  dol -

G                    D                              C
| - lars)     well, I'd | buy        you a  K  |- Car.    (A nice, | reliant  automobile.)      )|
  - lars)     well, I'd | buy you John  Merrick's re -| mains.  (All them| crazy     elephant bones.) }|
  - lars)     well, I'd   buy        you a  mon  - key.  (Haven't  you always wanted a  monkey?))

G                    D                              C
|                And if  I  | had  a  million  dol |- lars,      I'd |buy   your    love.   |
```

To Coda ⊕

```
D
|                 |               |               |               ‖
```

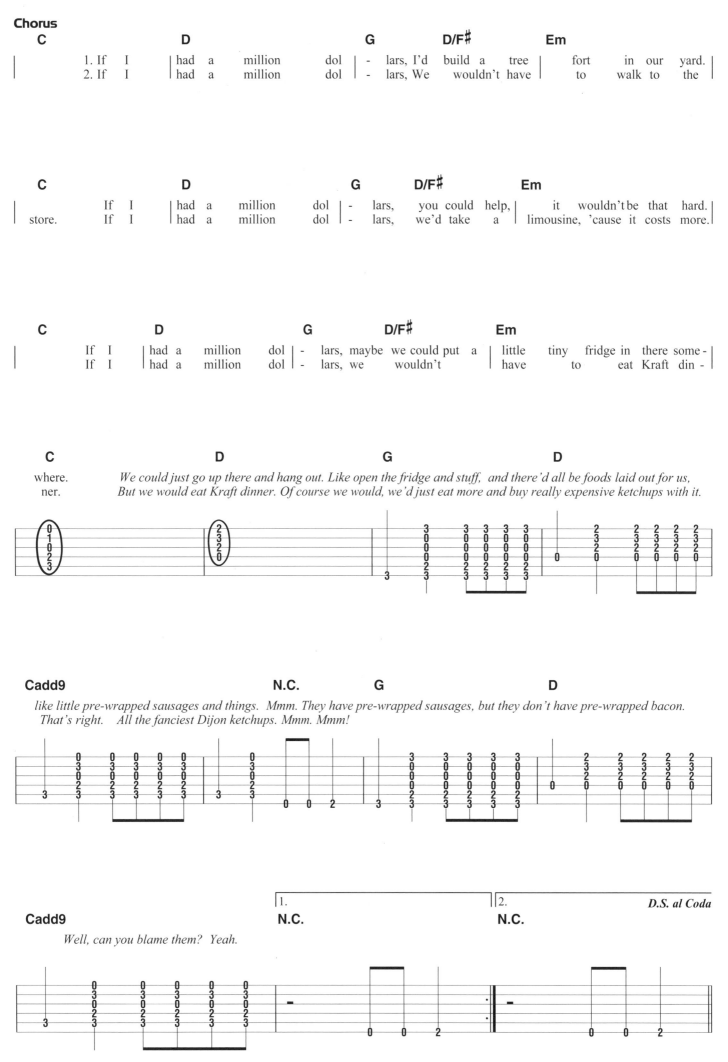

⊕ Coda

Outro-Chorus

C		D		G	D/F♯	

If I | had a million dol | - lars, if I |

Em		C		D	

| had a million dol - | lars, if I | had a million dol - |

G	D/F♯	Em		C	

| - lars, if I | had a million dol - | lars, if I | |

D		G	D/F♯	Em	C	

| had a million dol | - | lars, | |

Freely

D	G	C	G

I'd be rich.

let ring

The Joker

Words and Music by Steve Miller, Eddie Curtis and Ahmet Ertegun

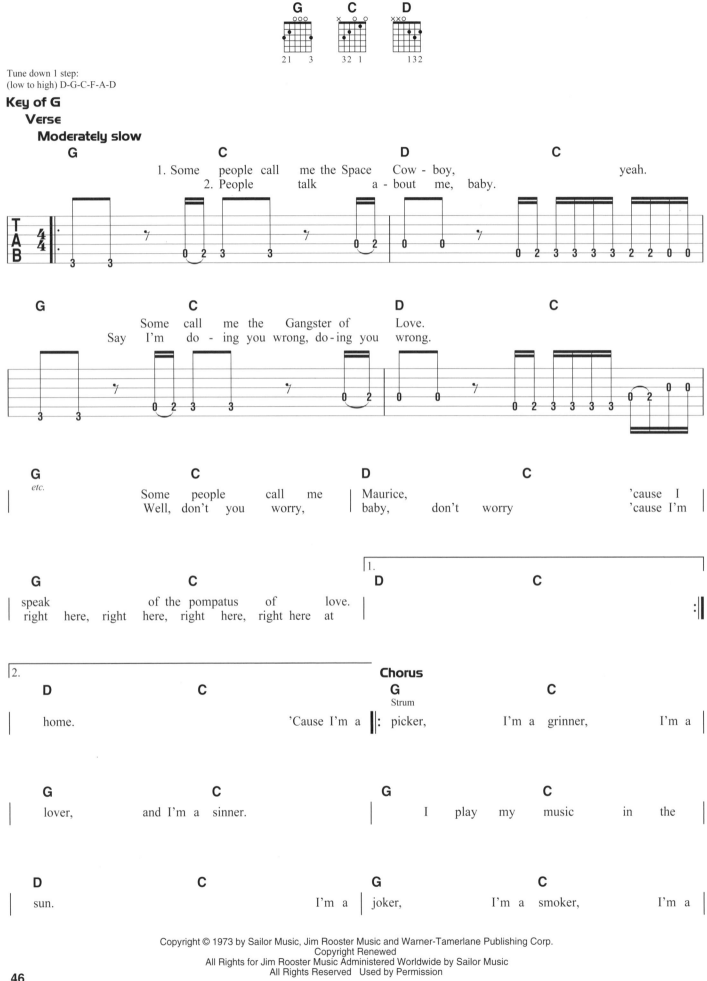

Tune down 1 step:
(low to high) D-G-C-F-A-D

Key of G

Verse

Moderately slow

G **C**	**G** **C**
midnight toker.	⎧ I sure don't want to hurt no
	⎩ I get my loving on the

|1. |2.
| **D**   **C** | **D**
| one.   I'm a   :‖| run.   Ooh, hoo. | Ooh, hoo.   ‖

Verse

| **G**   **C**   **D**   **C**
| w/ Verse pattern
| 3. You're   the   cutest   thing   that   I   ev | -   er   did   see.   I |

| **G**   **C**   **D**   **C**
| really   love   your   peaches,   want   to | shake   your   tree. |

| **G**   **C**   **D**   **C**
| Lovey   dovey, lovey dovey, lovey | dovey, all   the   time. |

| **G**   **C**   **D**   **C**
| Ooh,   wee,   baby,   I'll   sure show | you a good   time.   'Cause I'm a ‖

Chorus

| **G**   **C**   **G**   **C**
| Strum
|‖: picker,   I'm a   grinner,   I'm a | lover,   and I'm a   sinner. |

| **G**   **C**   **D**   **C**
| I   play   my   music   in   the | sun.   I'm a |

| **G**   **C**   **G**   **C**
| joker,   I'm a   smoker,   I'm a | midnight   toker. |

Repeat and fade

| **G**   **C**   **D**   **C**
| I   get   my   loving   on   the | run.   I'm a :‖
| I   sure   don't   want   to   hurt   no | one.

Lake of Fire

Words and Music by Curt Kirkwood

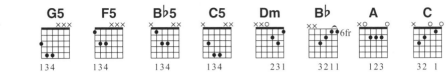

Tune down 1/2 step:
(low to high) E♭-A♭-D♭-G♭-B♭-E♭

Key of Gm
Intro
   Moderately

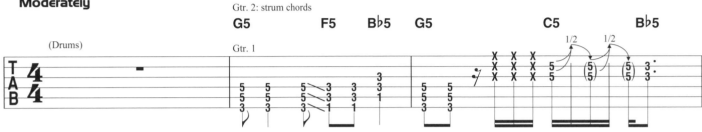

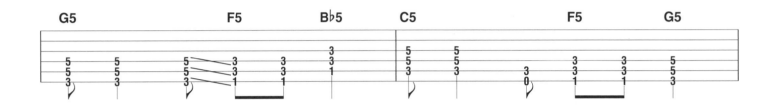

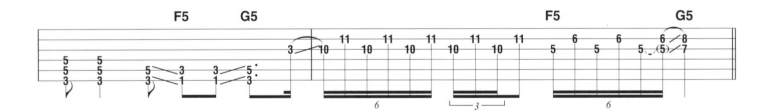

℅ Chorus

Gtr. 1: w/ Intro pattern

| G5 | | F5 | B♭5 | G5 | | C5 | B♭5 |

‖: Where do bad folks go when they die? They | don't go to heav-en where the an-gels fly. |

To Coda ⊕

| G5 | | F5 | B♭5 | C5 | | F5 | G5 |

| Go to a lake of fire and fry. | See 'em a-gain till the Fourth of Ju-ly. |

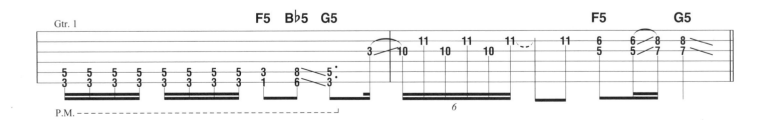

Verse

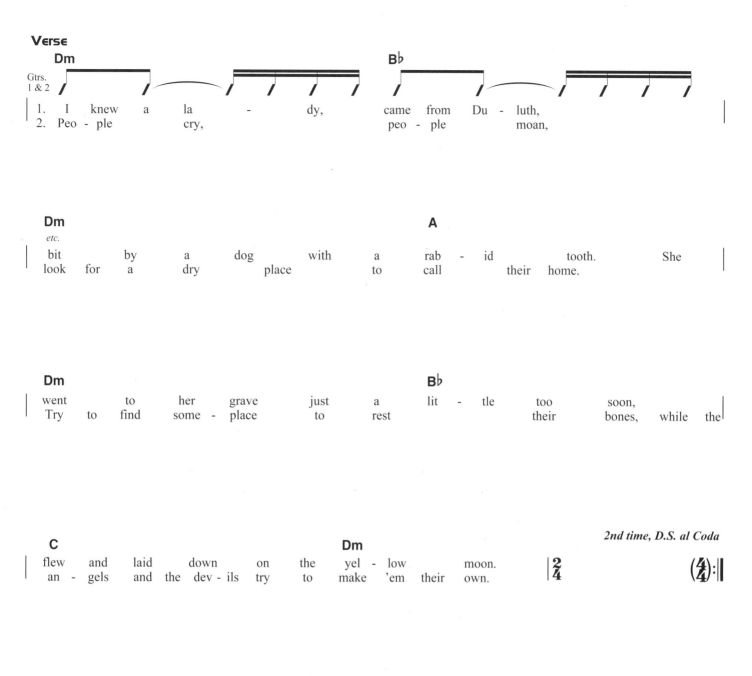

Dm
1. I knew a la - dy, came from Du - luth,
2. Peo - ple cry, peo - ple moan,

Gtrs.
1 & 2

Bb

Dm
bit by a dog with a rab - id tooth. She
look for a dry place to call their home.
etc.

A

Dm
went to her grave just a lit - tle too soon,
Try to find some - place just to rest their bones, while the

Bb

C
flew and laid down on the yel - low moon.
an - gels and the dev - ils try to make 'em their own.

Dm

|2/4| (|4/4| :||)

2nd time, D.S. al Coda

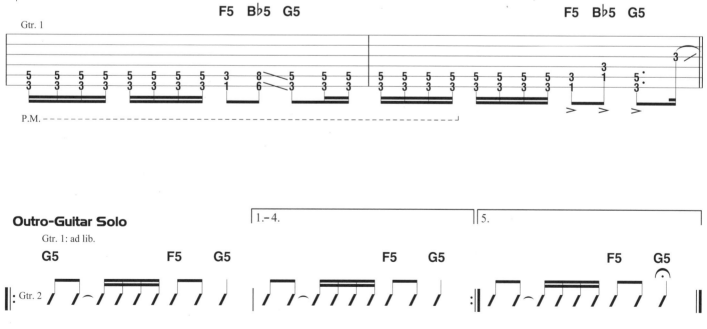

Coda

F5 Bb5 G5   F5 Bb5 G5

Gtr. 1

P.M. -

Outro-Guitar Solo

Gtr. 1: ad lib.

|1.–4.| |5.|

G5   F5   G5   F5   G5   F5   G5

Gtr. 2

The Lazy Song

Words and Music by Bruno Mars, Ari Levine, Philip Lawrence and Keinan Warsame

| **E** | | **B** | **F#** |

\- y - thing.   I just wan - na lay in my bed.

| **E** | | **B** | **F#** |

Don't | feel like pick - in' up my phone, so

| **E** | | **B** | **D#7** |

leave a mes - sage at the tone 'cause to - | day I swear I'm not do - in' an -

1.

w/ Chorus pattern

| **E** | | **B** | **F#** |

\- y - thing, noth - in' at all. | Woo, hoo, woo, hoo,

| **E** | | **B** | **F#** | *To Coda* ⊕

hoo. Noth - in' at all. | Woo, hoo, woo, hoo,

| **E** | | **2.** **E** |

hoo. 2. To - mor - row : ‖ - y - thing. No, I

Bridge

w/ Chorus pattern

| **C#m** | **F#*** | **G#m** |

ain't gon - na comb my hair 'cause | I ain't go - in' an - y - where,

| **C#m** | **F#*** | **G#m** |

no, no, no, no, no, no, no, no, no, | oh. I'll just

| **C#m** | **F#*** | **G#m** |

strut in my birth - day suit and let | ev - 'ry - thing hang loose,

D.S. al Coda
(take 1st ending)

| **C#m** | **F#*** | **G#m** **N.C.** |

yeah, yeah, yeah, yeah, yeah, yeah, yeah, yeah, yeah, | yeah. Oh, to -

⊕ Coda

| **E** | **N.C.** |

hoo. Noth - ing at all. |

Learning to Fly

Words and Music by Tom Petty and Jeff Lynne

F   C   Am   G

3211   32 1   231   32   4

Key of C
Intro
Moderately

1., 2., 3.   4.

F   C   Am   G   Am   G   1. Well, I

℅ Verse

F	C	Am	G	F	C	Am	G

etc.
started out / (3.) some say life   down a / will   dir-ty / beat you   road, / down   and

start-ed out / break your heart,   all a-/steal your lone. / crown.   And the / So I've

sun went down / start-ed out   as I / for crossed the / God knows hill. / where.   And the / I

town lit up, / guess I'll know   the / when world got / I get still. / there.   I'm / I'm

Chorus

learn-ing to fly / learn-ing to fly   but I / a-round ain't got / the clouds. wings.

Com-ing down / What goes up   (Learn-ing to fly.)   is the / must hard-est come thing. / down.   _To Coda_ ⊕   2. Well, the

Verse

good old days   may / not re-turn   and the

rocks might melt   and the / sea may burn.   I'm

Chorus

| F | C | Am | G | F | C | Am | G |

learn-ing to fly | (Learn-ing to fly.) | but I | ain't got wings. | (Learn-ing to fly.) |

| F | C | Am | G | F | C |

Com-ing down | (Learn-ing to fly.) | is the | hard - est thing. |

| Am | G |

(Learn-ing to fly.) |

Guitar Solo

| F | C |

1., 2., 3.

| Am | G |

4.

D.S. al Coda

| Am | G |

3. Well,

⊕ Coda

| Am | G |

Interlude

| F | C |

1.

Shouted: Ay! | Am | G |

2.

etc.

4. I'm

Chorus

w/ Intro pattern

| F | C | Am | G | F | C |

learn-ing to fly | (Learn-ing to fly.) | but I | ain't got wings. |
| | | | a- | round the clouds. |

| Am | G | F | C | Am | G |

| Com-ing down | (Learn-ing to fly.) | is the |
| What goes up |

1.

| F | C | Am | G |

| hard - est thing. | I'm |
| must come down. |

2.

| Am | G |

I'm

Outro

| F | C | Am | G | F | C | Am | G |

1.

learn-ing to fly. | (Learn-ing to fly. | | Learn-ing to fly.) | I'm |

2.

Repeat and fade

| Am | G | F | C | Am | G |

Learn-ing to fly.) | | (Learn-ing to fly.) |

Leaving on a Jet Plane

Words and Music by John Denver

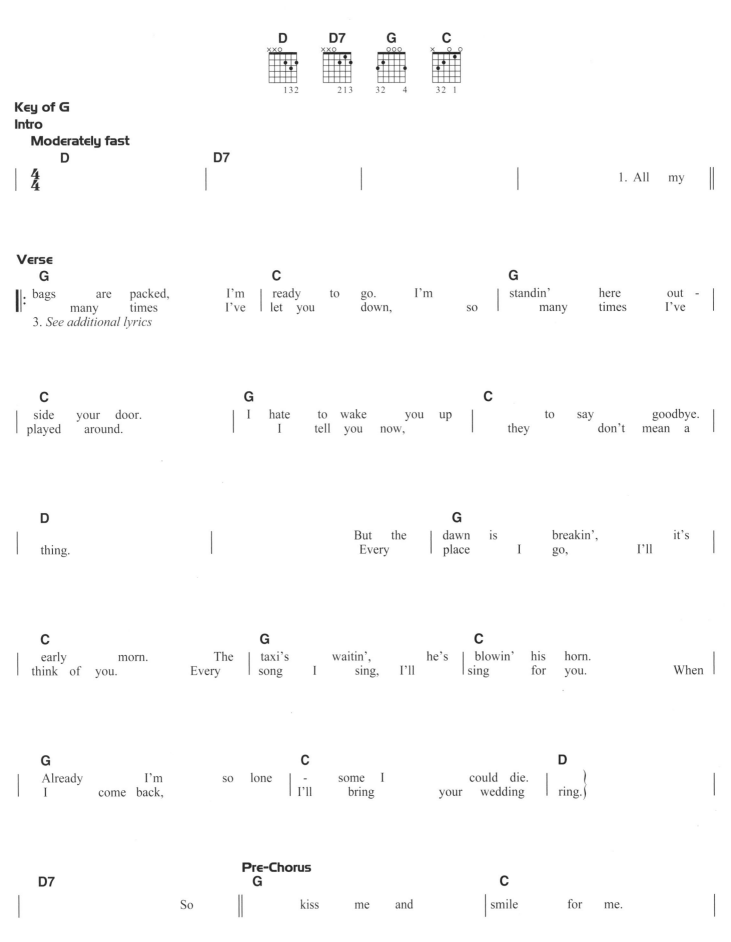

Key of G

Intro

Moderately fast

| D | | | D7 | | | | 1. All my ||

Verse

G ‖: bags are packed, I'm |C ready to go. I'm |G standin' here out- |
many times I've let you down, so many times I've
3. See additional lyrics

C | side your door. |G I hate to wake you up |C to say goodbye. |
played around. I tell you now, they don't mean a

D | thing. | G But the | dawn is breakin', it's |
Every place I go, I'll

C | early morn. The |G taxi's waitin', he's |C blowin' his horn. When |
think of you. Every song I sing, I'll sing for you.

G | Already I'm so lone |C -some I could die. |D }|
I come back, I'll bring your wedding ring.}

Pre-Chorus

D7 | So ‖G kiss me and |C smile for me. |

G				C			G		
Tell	me	that	you'll	wait	for	me.	Hold	me	like	you'll

C				D			D7			
never		let	me	go.					'Cause	I'm

Chorus

G			C				G			
leav	-	in'	on	a	jet	plane;	don't	know	when	I'll

C				G			C			
	be	back	again.			Oh, babe,		I	hate	to

‖1., 2.

D						D7				
go.									2. There's	so :‖

‖3.

Outro

D7			G			C			
		I'm	leav	-	in'	on	a	jet	plane;

G				C			G		
	don't	know	when	I'll	be	back	again.		Oh,

C				D			
babe,			I	hate	to	go.	

D7			D	D7	G	

Additional Lyrics

3. Now the time has come to leave you.
One more time, let me kiss you.
Then close your eyes and I'll be on my way.
Dream about the days to come
When I won't have to leave alone,
About the times I won't have to say:

Let Her Cry

Words and Music by Darius Rucker, Dean Felber, Mark Bryan and Jim Sonefeld

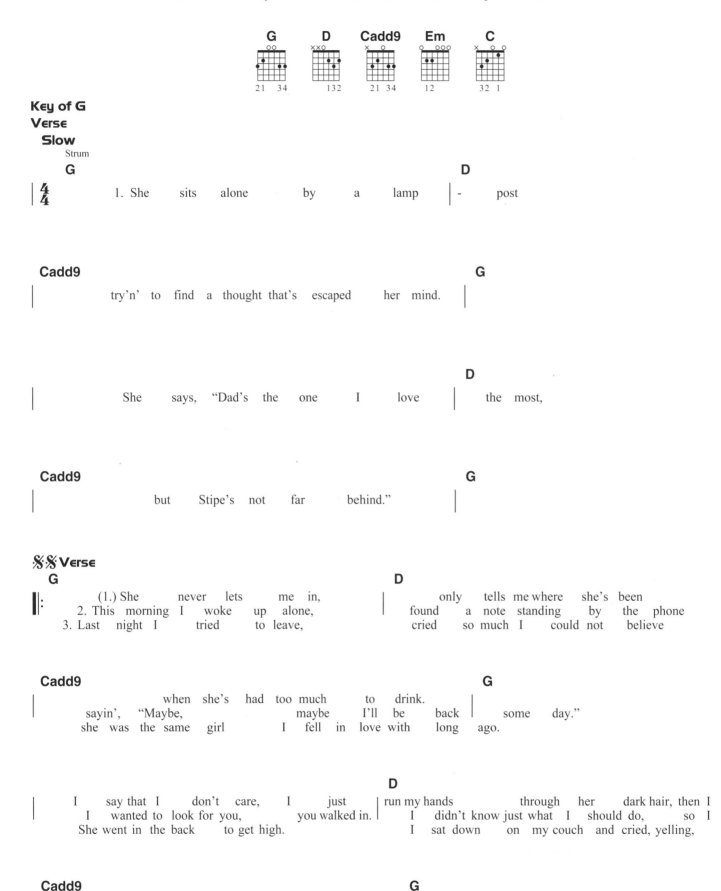

Key of G
Verse
Slow

Strum

|G| 4/4 | 1. She sits alone by a lamp -post | **D** |

Cadd9 | try'n' to find a thought that's escaped her mind. | **G** |

| She says, "Dad's the one I love the most, | **D** |

Cadd9 | but Stipe's not far behind." | **G** | |

𝄋𝄋 Verse

|G|
‖: | (1.) She never lets me in, | **D** | only tells me where she's been |
| 2. This morning I woke up alone, | | found a note standing by the phone |
| 3. Last night I tried to leave, | | cried so much I could not believe |

Cadd9
| when she's had too much to drink. | **G** |
| sayin', "Maybe, maybe I'll be back | some day." |
| she was the same girl I fell in love with long ago. |

I say that I don't care, I just	**D**	run my hands through her dark hair, then I
I wanted to look for you, you walked in.		I didn't know just what I should do, so I
She went in the back to get high.		I sat down on my couch and cried, yelling,

Cadd9
| pray to God you gotta help me fly away. | **G** | And just ⎫|
| sat back down and had a beer and felt | sorry for myself. Sayin' ⎬ let her cry ‖
| "Oh, mama, please help me. | Won't you hold my hand?" And ⎭|

% Chorus

Cadd9 ... G ... Cadd9

if the | tears fall down like rain. ... Let her sing | ... if it |

4th time, To Coda 2 ⊕

Em ... G ... D ... Cadd9 ... G

eases all her pain. ... Let her go, | ... let her | walk right out on me. ... And if the |

Guitar Solo

D ... C ... G ... D

sun comes up tomorrow, let her be, | ... let her be. ‖ ... |

3rd time, To Coda 1 ⊕ | 1. ... | 2.

Cadd9 ... G ... G

| ... | ... :‖ ... |

D.S. al Coda 1 ... ⊕ **Coda 1** ... *D.S.S. al Coda 2*

D ... Cadd9 ... G ... G

| ... | ... | ... Let her cry ‖ ... | ... ‖

⊕ **Coda 2**

D ... G

| sun comes up tomorrow, ... let her be. | ... Let her cry ‖

Chorus

Cadd9 ... G ... Cadd9

if the | tears fall down like rain. ... Let her sing | ... if it |

Em ... G ... D ... Cadd9 ... G

eases all her pain. ... Let her go, | ... let her | walk right out on me. ... And if the |

D ... C ... G

| sun comes up tomorrow, let her be. | ... Ah, let her be. | ... ‖

Little Black Submarines

Words and Music by Dan Auerbach, Patrick Carney and Brian Burton

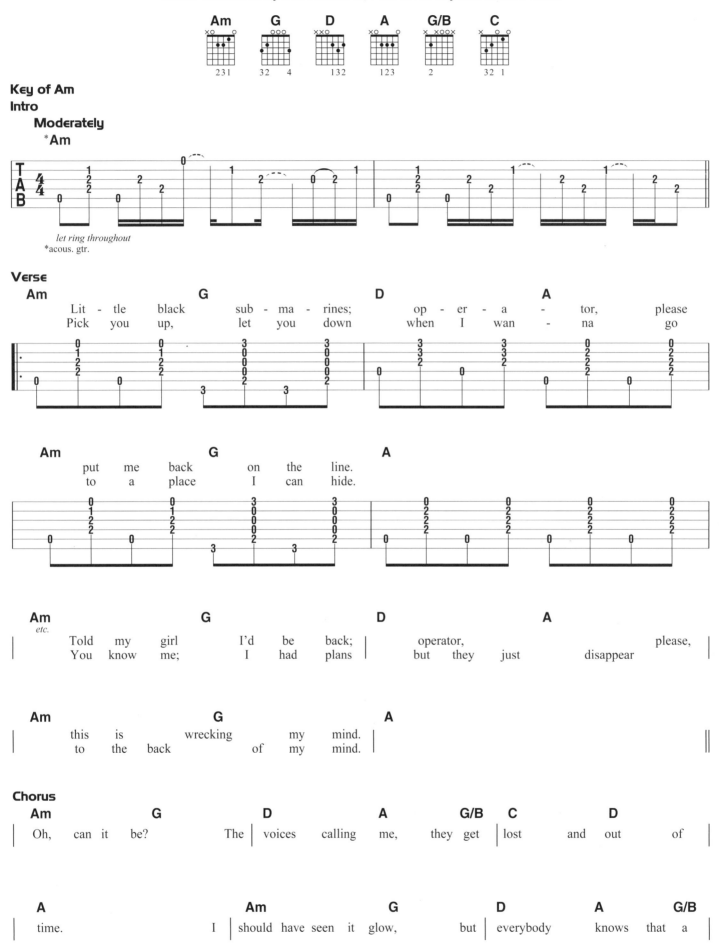

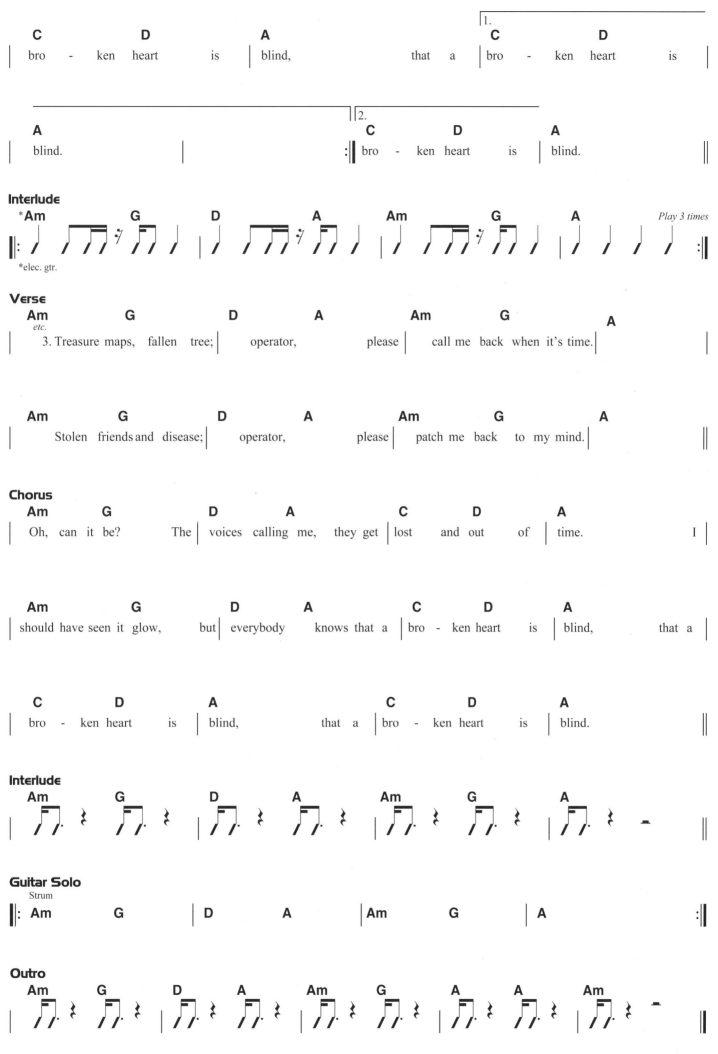

C	D	A		C	D
bro - ken heart is	blind,	that a	bro - ken heart is

1.

A			C	D	A
blind.		bro - ken heart is	blind.

2.

Interlude

Am G D A Am G A *Play 3 times*

elec. gtr.

Verse

Am G D A Am G A
etc.

bro - ken heart is 3.Treasure maps, fallen tree; operator, please call me back when it's time.

Am G D A Am G A

Stolen friends and disease; operator, please patch me back to my mind.

Chorus

Am G D A C D A

Oh, can it be? The voices calling me, they get lost and out of time. I

Am G D A C D A

should have seen it glow, but everybody knows that a bro - ken heart is blind, that a

C D A C D A

bro - ken heart is blind, that a bro - ken heart is blind.

Interlude

Am G D A Am G A

Guitar Solo

Strum

Am G | D A | Am G | A |

Outro

Am G D A Am G A A Am

59

Lucky

Words and Music by Jason Mraz, Colbie Caillat and Timothy Fagan

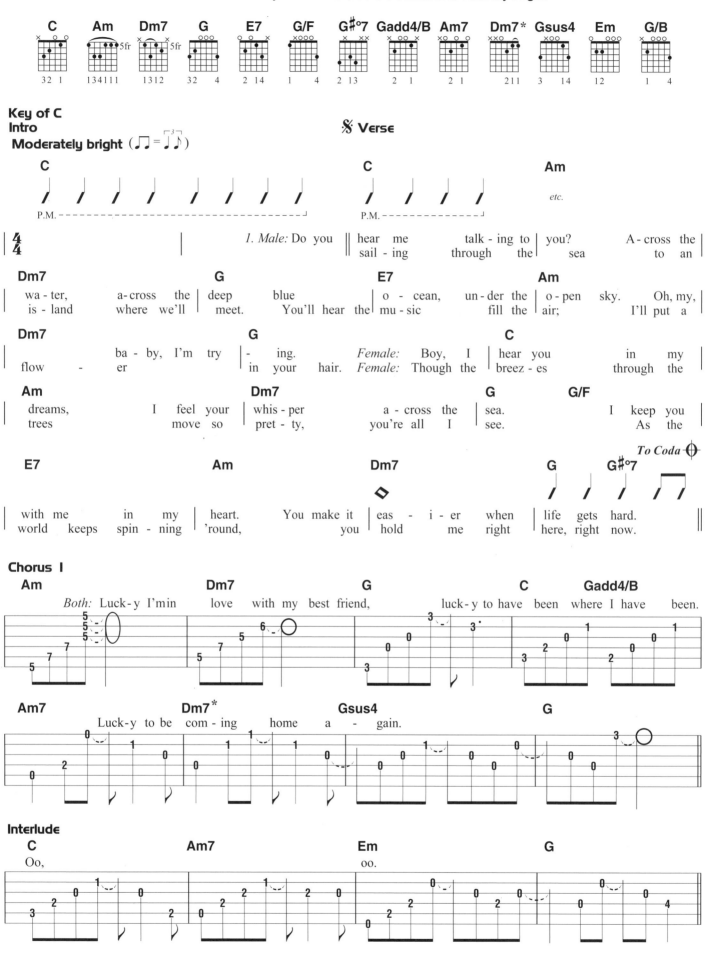

Bridge

Dm7   / / / /   *etc.*   Am7   G   Dm7

| *Female:* They don't know how | long it takes, | wait-ing for a | love like this. |
| *Male:* They don't | know how long it | takes, | wait-ing for a | love like this. |

            Am7   G   Dm7

| Ev - 'ry time we | say good - bye, | | *Both:* I wish we had | one more kiss. I'll |
| Ev - 'ry | time we say good - | bye, | | | |

            Am7   G   Am7   G/B

| wait for you, I | prom - ise you I | will. | I'm |

Chorus 2

w/ Chorus pattern

Am   Dm7   G   C   Gadd4/B

| luck - y I'm in | love with my best friend, | luck - y to have | been where I have been. |

Am7   Dm7 *   Gsus4   G   G#°7

| Luck - y to be | com - ing home a | - gain. | |

Am   Dm7   G   C   Gadd4/B

| Luck-y we're in | love in ev -'ry way, | luck - y to have | stayed where we have stayed. |

D.S. al Coda

Am7   Dm7 *   Gsus4   G

| Luck - y to be | com - ing home some | - day. | 2. *Male:* And so I'm |

⊕ Coda

Chorus 2 (1 time)   **Outro**

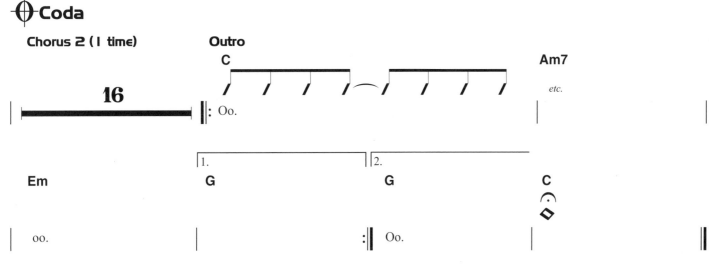

Em   1. G   2. G   C

| oo. | | Oo. |

Man on the Moon

Words and Music by William Berry, Peter Buck, Michael Mills and Michael Stipe

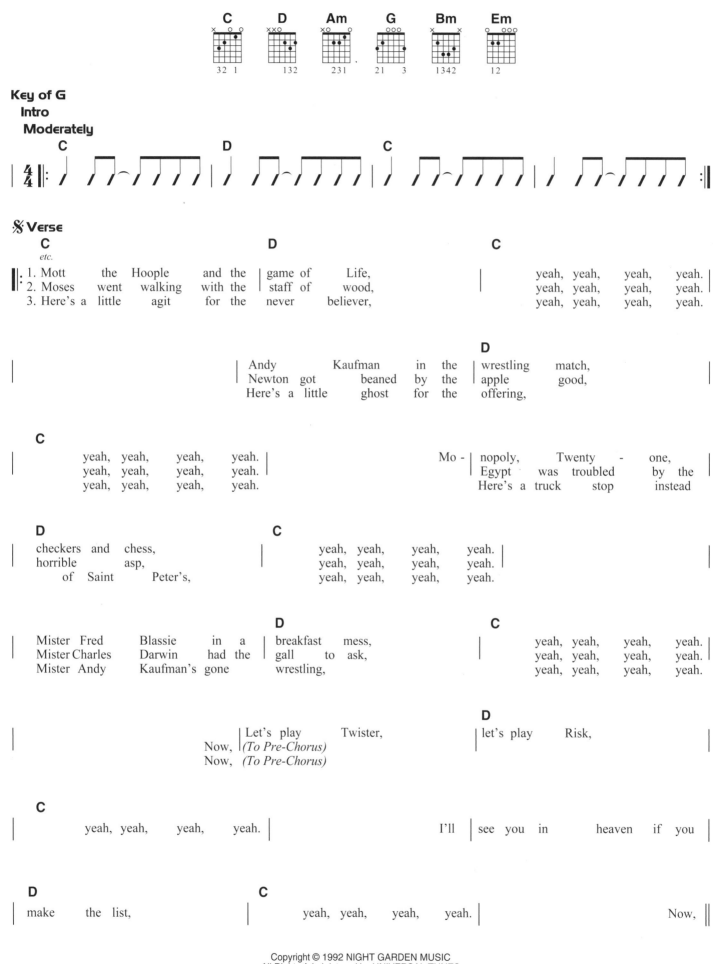

Pre-Chorus

Strum

| Am | | | G | | Am | | | G |
| If you believe | | | | | | | | |

Andy, did you hear about this | one? | Tell me are you locked in the punch? |

| Am | | G | C | D |

Andy, are you goofing on El | - vis? Hey, baby, | { 1., 3. are we losing   touch? |
{ 2. are you having   fun? ‖

Chorus

| G | Am | C | Bm |

If you believe | they put a man on the moon, |

| G | Am | D | | G | Am |

man on the moon. | If you believe |

| C | Bm | Am |

there's nothing up their sleeve, | then nothing is cool. | :‖

Interlude

Em   D   Em   D

To Coda ⊕   *D.S al Coda*   ⊕ **Coda**
                   (no repeat)

Em   D

Outro-Chorus

Strum

| G | Am | C | Bm | G | Am |

‖: If you believe | they put a man on the moon, | man on the moon. |

| D | G | Am | C | Bm |

If you believe | there's nothing up their sleeve, |

| Am | Em |

Play 3 times

then nothing is cool. | :‖

63

Midnight Rider

Words and Music by Gregg Allman and Robert Kim Payne

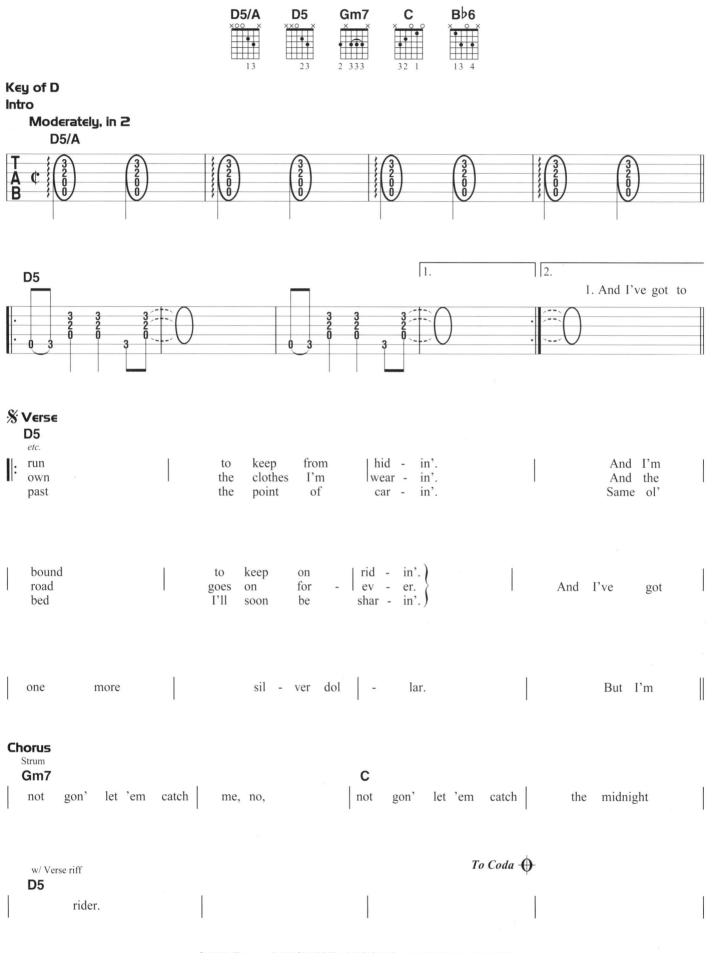

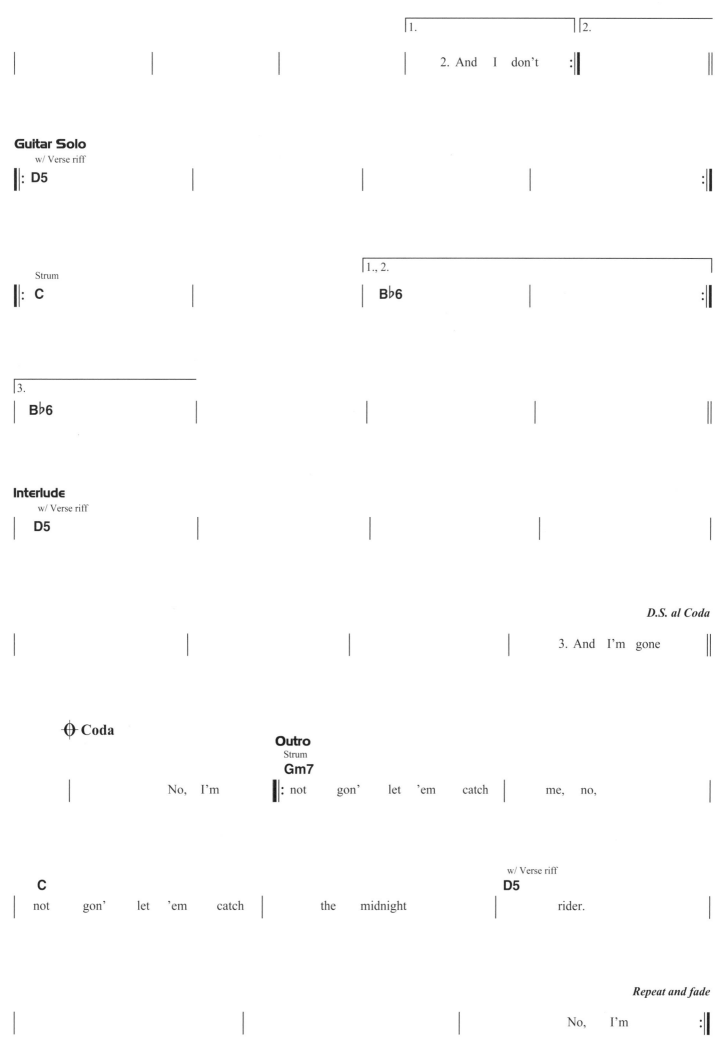

Mr. Jones

Words and Music by Adam Duritz, David Bryson, Charles Gillingham,
Matthew Malley, Steve Bowman, Daniel Vickrey and Ben Mize

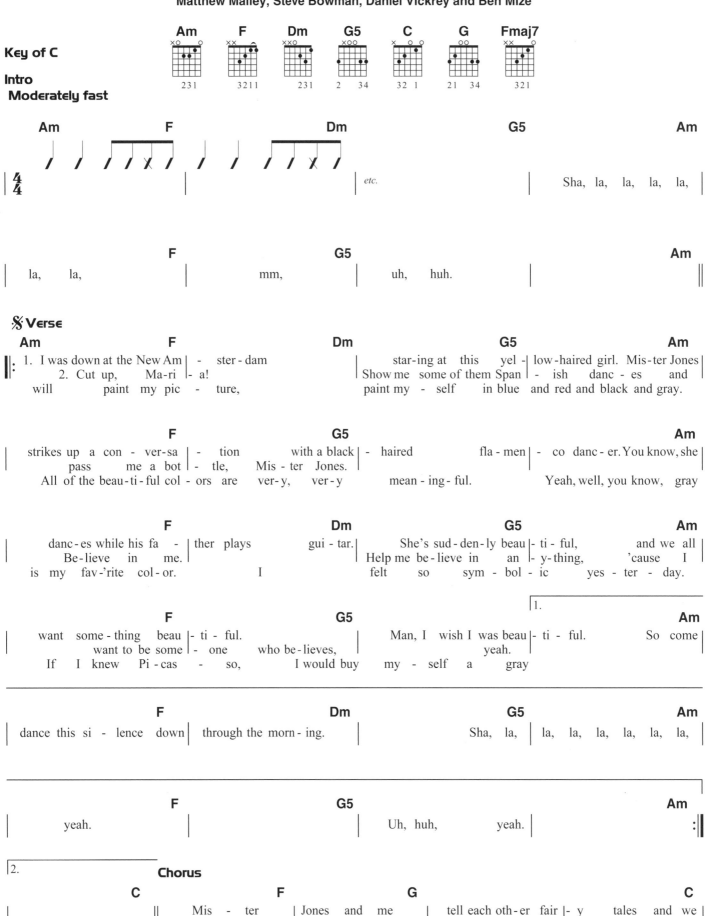

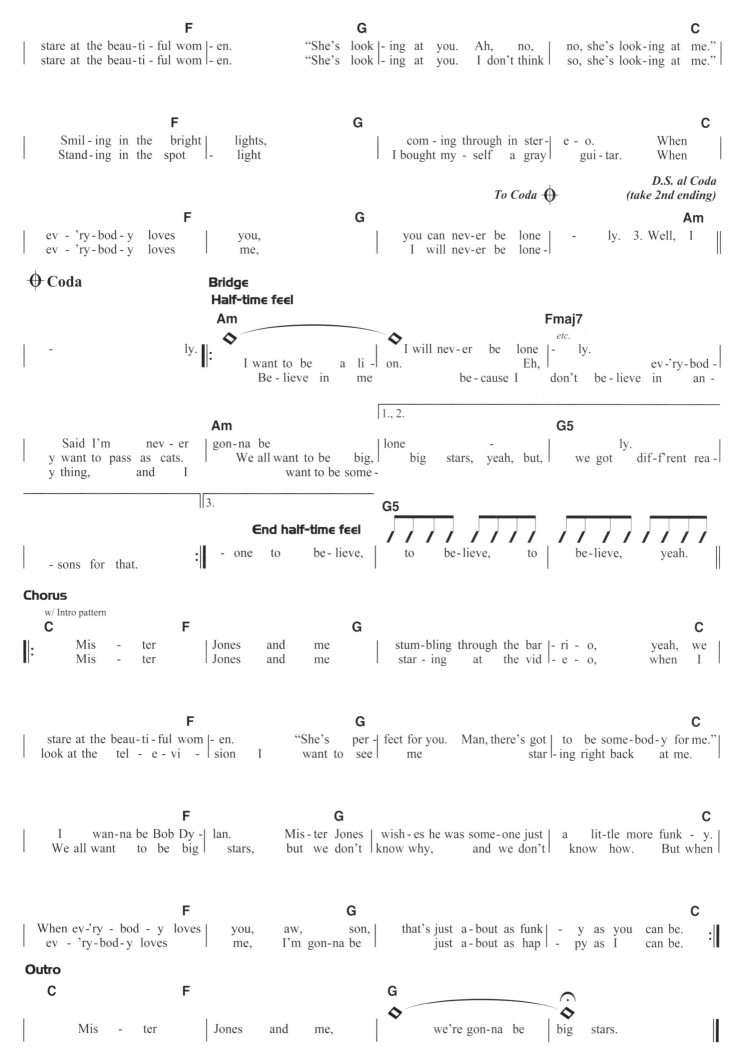

Night Moves

Words and Music by Bob Seger

G F C/G D Em Cmaj7/G G7

Capo I

Key of A♭ (Capo Key of G)

Intro

Moderately

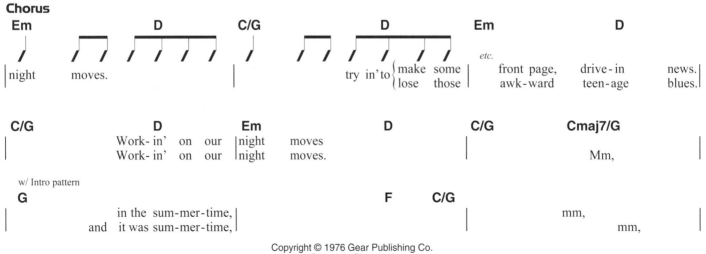

Verse

G
:|| 1. I was a lit-tle too tall, could 've used a | few   pounds.

F   C/G

Tight pants, points,   hard |- ly re - nown.

||: She was a black-haired beau-ty with big,
3. We weren't in love,   oh |

F   G

dark   eyes   and points   all her own   sit-tin' | way   up   high,
no, far from   it.   We weren't search - in' for some pie - | in-the-sky   sum - mit.

F   G

F   C/G

We were just   young and   rest - | less and bored,   way up   firm   and high.
liv-in' by   the sword.

F   C/G

Verse

F   G   G
|| 2. Out past the corn-fields, where the | woods   got heav-y,
|| 4. And we'd steal   a-way   ev -'ry | chance we could

F   C/G

out   in the back seat   of my six | - ty Chev-y,   work-in' on mys-t'ries with-out
to the back room,   to the al ley, or the | trust - y   woods.   I used her, she used me, but nei-

F   G

an-y clues.   We were get-tin' our share.}   Work-in' on our
-ther one   cared.

F   C/G

D

Chorus

Em   D   C/G   D   Em   D

night   moves.   try in'to {make some   front page,   drive-in   news.
                                     lose those   awk-ward   teen-age   blues.

C/G   D   Em   D   C/G   Cmaj7/G

Work-in' on our | night   moves
Work-in' on our | night   moves.   Mm,

w/ Intro pattern
G   F   C/G

in the sum-mer-time,   mm,
and   it was sum-mer-time,   mm,

| F   G | in the sweet | sum - mer - time.   F   C/G |
| | sweet | sum - mer-time,   sum - mer-time. |

|1. | F   G :|| |2.   D ||

Interlude

Em   D   G   G7

|◇   ⌐. |♪ / / / / / |◇ | |◇ | And ||

Bridge
w/ Chorus pattern

Cmaj7/G   **G**

| oh, | the | won-der. | |

Cmaj7/G   **F**

| We felt the light-ning, | yeah, | and we wait-ed on   the thun-|

                              D   **G**
                                                                          ⌢
| der, | wait-ed on the thun-der.| |◇ ||

Verse
Free time

*G   Cmaj7/G

| 5. I a-woke last night to the sound of thun-der.   How far off,   I sat and won-dered. |
*Let chords ring, next 11 meas.

G   Cmaj7/G

| Start-ed hum-ming a song from nine-teen six-ty-two.   Ain't it fun - ny   how   the   night |

Em   C/G

| moves   when you just   don't   seem   to have |

Em   C/G   Em

| as much to lose?   Strange   how   the night moves |

C/G   Cmaj7/G   G
                                                              ⌢
| with au-tumn clos - ing in. |◇ ||

Interlude
A tempo
w/ Intro pattern

||: G | F   C/G | | F   G :||

Outro
w/ Lead Voc. ad lib.
Repeat and fade

G   F   C/G   F   G

||:(Night moves. | | Night moves.) | :||

Norwegian Wood
(This Bird Has Flown)

Words and Music by John Lennon and Paul McCartney

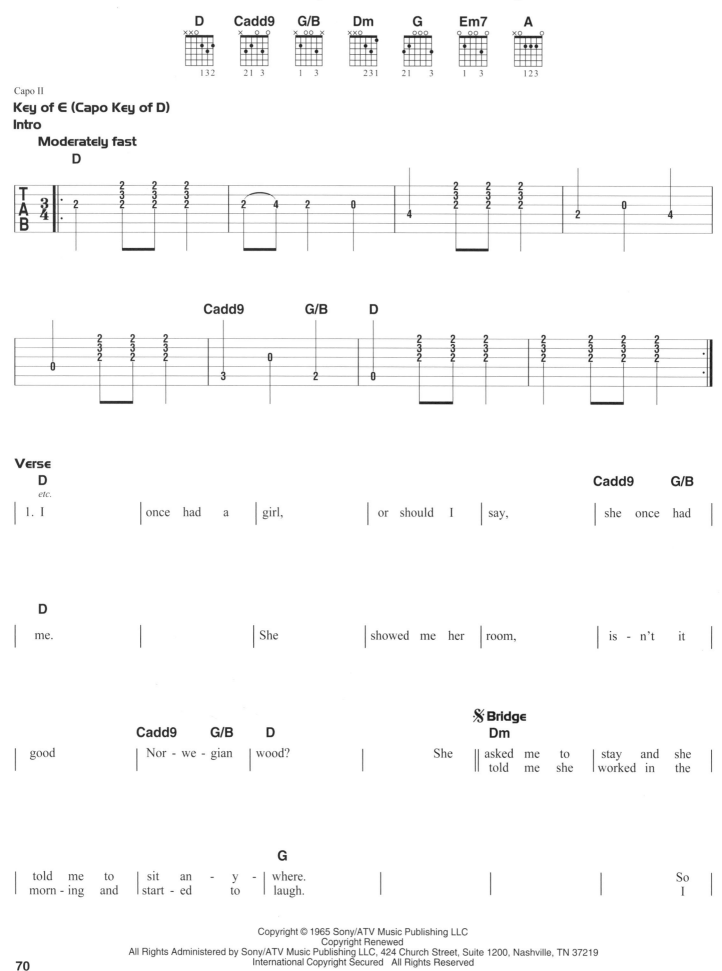

Capo II

Key of E (Capo Key of D)
Intro

Moderately fast

Verse

D

1. I | once had a | girl, | or should I | say, | she once had |

D

| me. | | She | showed me her | room, | is - n't it |

| good | Nor - we - gian | wood? | | She | asked me to | stay and she |
| | | | | | told me she | worked in the |

G

| told me to | sit an - y - | where. | | | | So |
| morn - ing and | start - ed to | laugh. | | | | I |

Dm   **Em7**

| I looked a - | round and I | no - ticed there | was - n't a | chair. | | |
| told her I | did - n't and | crawled off to | sleep in the | bath. | | |

                                                   Verse

A   **D**

| | | 2. I | sat on a | rug, bid - ing my |
| | | 3. And | when I a - woke, I was a - |

                              Cadd9   **G/B**   **D**

| time, | drink - ing her | wine. | | We | talked un - til |
| lone; | this bird had | flown. | | So | I lit a |

                                                        To Coda ⊕

                              Cadd9   **G/B**   **D**

| two, | and then she | said, | "It's time for | bed." | | |
| fire; | is - n't it | good | Nor - we - gian | wood? | | |

Interlude

D

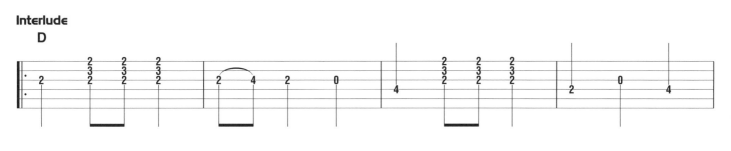

                                                        1.   2.   *D.S. al Coda*

Cadd9   **G/B**   **D**   She

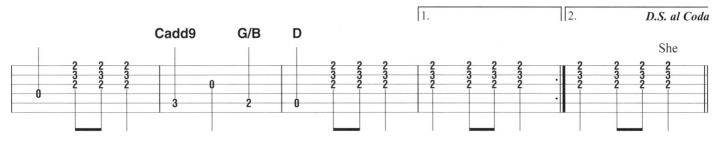

⊕ **Coda**

Outro

D

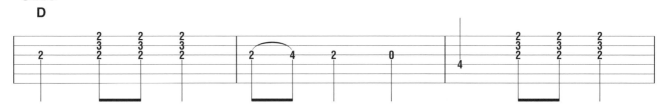

                                                           Cadd9   **G/B**   **D**

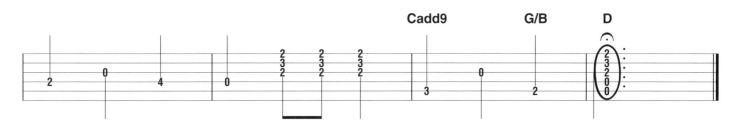

Renegades

Words and Music by Alexander Junior Grant, Adam Levin, Casey Harris, Noah Feldshuh and Samuel Harris

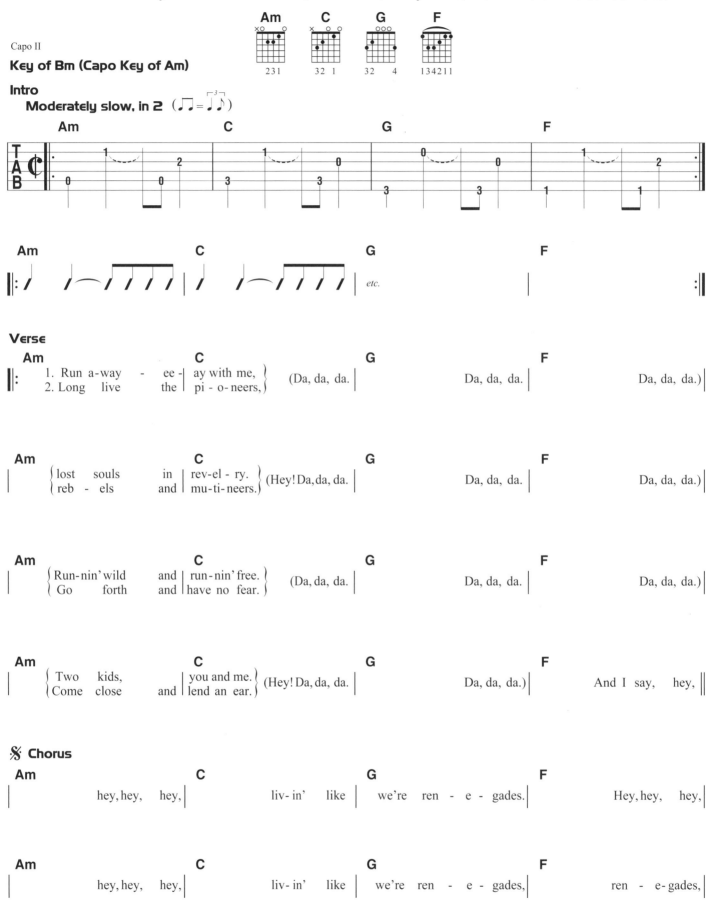

Capo II

Key of Bm (Capo Key of Am)

Intro
Moderately slow, in 2

Verse

1. Run a-way - ee - ay with me,
2. Long live the pi - o - neers,

(Da, da, da. Da, da, da. Da, da, da.)

{ lost souls in rev-el - ry.
{ reb - els and mu-ti-neers. } (Hey! Da, da, da. Da, da, da. Da, da, da.)

{ Run-nin' wild and run-nin' free.
{ Go forth and have no fear. } (Da, da, da. Da, da, da. Da, da, da.)

{ Two kids, you and me.
{ Come close and lend an ear. } (Hey! Da, da, da. Da, da, da.) And I say, hey,

Chorus

hey, hey, hey, liv-in' like we're ren - e - gades. Hey, hey, hey,

hey, hey, hey, liv-in' like we're ren - e - gades, ren - e - gades,

Am	C	G	F
(Oo.)			ren - e-gades.

3rd time, To Coda ⊕

Am	C	G	F
(Oo.)			:‖

Interlude

Am | C | G | F

```
Am                    C                    G                    F
  1                     1                    0                    1
     2                     0                       0                  2
0          0         3          3        3          3       1          1
```

Verse

Am	C	G	F
3. All hail the | un-der-dogs,	all hail the | new kids,	

Am	C	G	F
all hail the | out - laws,	Spiel - bergs and | Ku - bricks.	

Am	C	G	F
It's our time to | make a move,	it's our time to | make a-mends,	

D.S. al Coda

Am	C	G	F
it's our time to | break the rules.	Let's be - gin. | And I say, hey, ‖

⊕ **Coda**

Outro

‖: Am	C	G	F	:‖ F ‖

1. - 5. | 6.

Rhythm of Love

Words and Music by Tim Lopez

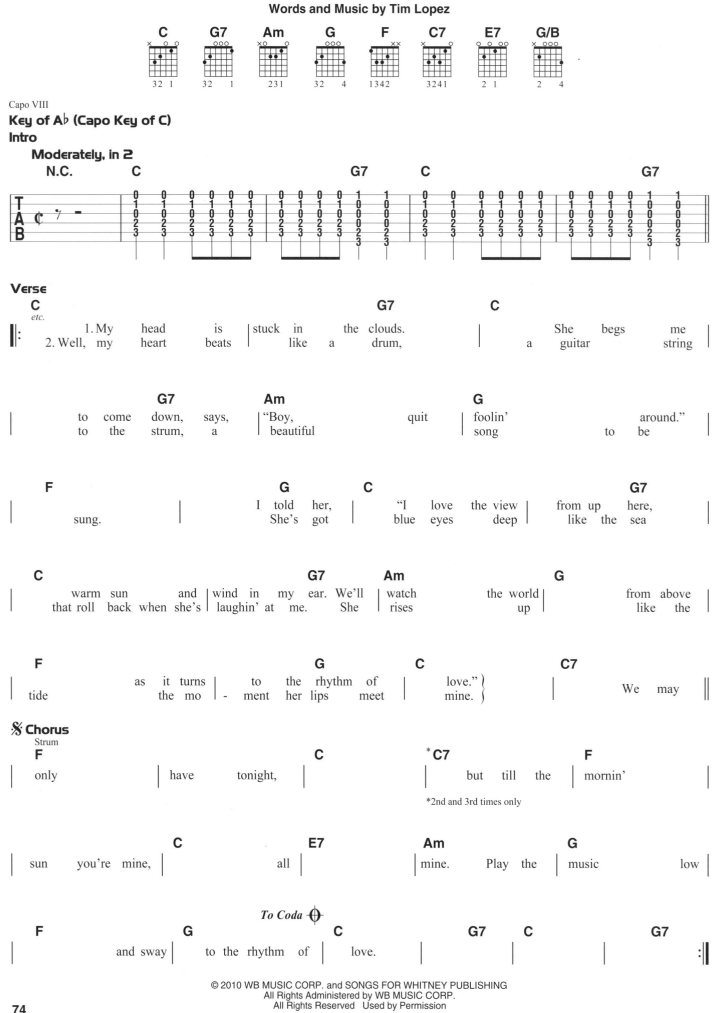

Bridge
Strum

E7	F	C	G/B
When the	moon is	low,	

E7	F	C	G/B
we can	dance in	slow	mo -

F		G	
- tion and	all your	tears	will sub -

F		G	
side.	All your	tears	will

Verse
Strum

C	G7	C	G7
*dry.			
3. Bop ba, bop	ba, bop ba.	Bop ba, bop	ba, bop ba.

*1st time only.

Am	G	F	G
Da, da, da,	dum, da, da,	dum.	

C	G7	C	
And long af	- ter I've gone,	you'll still be	

	G7	Am	G
humming along,	and	I will keep	you in my

D.S. al Coda

F	G	C	N.C.
mind, the way	you make love so	fine.	We may

⊕ **Coda**

C	G7	Am	G
love.	Oh,	play the	music low

F	G	C	G7
and sway	to the rhythm of	love.	

C	G7	C	G7	C
Yeah, sway	to the rhythm of	love.		

Runaway Train

Words and Music by David Pirner

C   C/B   Am   G   F   Em

Key of C

Intro
Moderately

C

```
T  4
A  4   3   5  5  5  5   5  3  3  3  3   2  2  2  3   2      1   1
B                                                           0 0   0    0
```
(tab: 5 5 5 / 3 3 3 / 1 1 / 0 / 1 1)

Verse

C   C/B
                                                                    etc.
1. Call you up   in the | mid-dle of the night | like a fire - fly with|-out   a   light. |
2. Can you help   me re- | mem-ber how to smile, | make it some-how all | seem worth - while? |

Am   G
| You were there like a | blow - torch burn - ing. | I   was a key   that could | use a lit-tle turn - ing. |
| How on earth did I | get   so   jad - ed? | Well, life's mys-ter-ies seem | so   fad - ed. |

C   C/B
| So   tired   that I |could-n't e - ven sleep. | So   man-y se-crets| I   could-n't keep. |
| I can go   where no | one else can go. | I   know what no | one else   knows. |

Am   G
| Prom-ised my - self | I   would-n't weep. | A, one   more   prom-ise | I   could-n't keep. It seems||
| Here I am just |drown-in' in the rain | with a tick-et for a |run-a-way   train. And ev - ||

Pre-Chorus

F   G   C   Am
| no   one   can help | me   now.   I'm in | too   deep,   there's no | way   out. |
| - 'ry - thing seems cut | and   dry.   Day| and   night,   earth| and   sky. |

F   Em   G
| This time   I   have | real-ly led   my - |self   a - stray. | ||
| Some-how I   just don't be - |lieve   it. | ||

𝄋 Chorus

C   Em
| Run-a-way   train, | nev-er go-ing back. | Wrong   way   on a | one - way   track. |

Am   G
| Seems   like   I should be | get - ting   some - where, | but some - how I'm neith - er |

© 1992 STANDING WATER MUSIC
All Rights Administered by WB MUSIC CORP.
All Rights Reserved   Used by Permission

76

3rd time, To Coda ⊕ |1.

| here | nor | there. | | | | ♪ | 𝄽 | ‒ | | :‖

|2.

Guitar Solo

| C | | | Em | | |

| Am | | | G | | |

| F | | G | C | | Am | |

| F | | Em | G | | ‖

Verse

C   C/B
◊ _____ ◊   *etc.*
| 3. Bought a tick-et for a | run-a-way   train | | like a mad - man | laugh-in' at the rain. |

                                                                              D.S. al Coda
Am   G
| A lit-tle out of touch, | lit-tle in - sane. | It's just   eas - i - er than | deal-ing with the pain. ‖

⊕ **Coda**

C
| Run-a - way train, nev | - er com-in' back. | Run-a - way train tear | - in' up the track. |

Am   G
| Run-a - way train burn | - in' in my veins. | A, run-a-way,   but it | al-ways seems the same. ‖

Outro

‖: C | | C/B | |

                                                                              Repeat and fade
| Am | | G | | :‖

The Scientist

Words and Music by Guy Berryman, Jon Buckland, Will Champion and Chris Martin

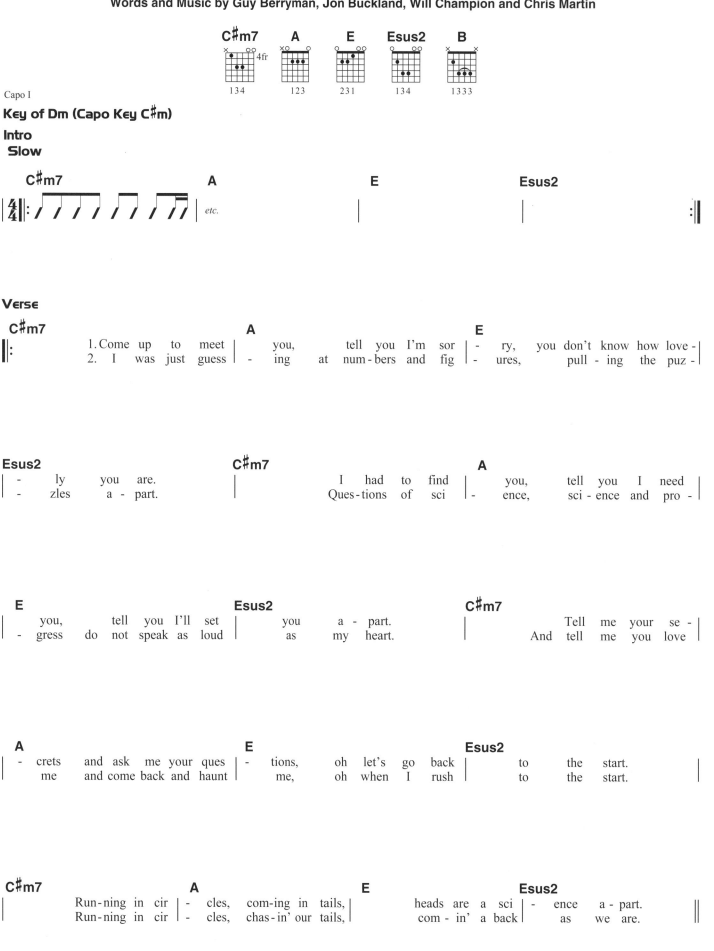

Chorus

A   E

| No - bod-y said | it was eas - y, | it's such a shame |

Esus2   A   E

| for us to part. | No - bod-y said | it was eas - y, | no one ev-er |

                              B

| said it would be { this hard. / so hard. } | ◇ Oh, take me back to the start. / I'm go-in' back to the start. ‖

Interlude

| E | A | E | |

| C#m7 | A | E |【1.】Esus2 :‖ 【2.】 ‖

Outro

C#m7   A   E   *Play 3 times*

‖: | Ah, oo, | oo, oo, oo, | oo. | :‖

C#m7   A   E

◇   ◇   ◇

| Ah, oo, | oo, oo, oo, | oo. ‖

Shallow
from A STAR IS BORN

Words and Music by Stefani Germanotta, Mark Ronson, Andrew Wyatt and Anthony Rossomando

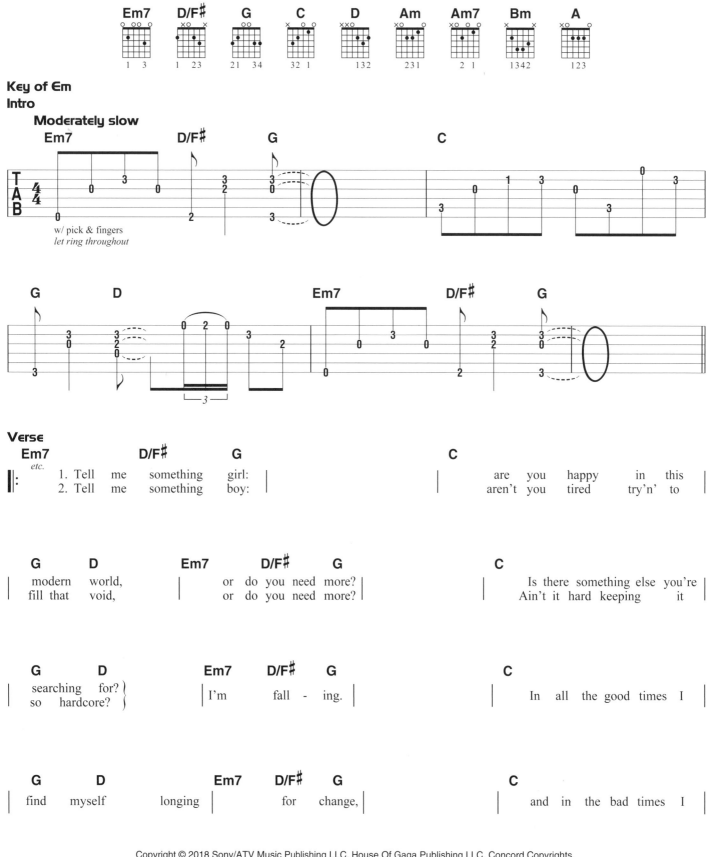

1.

Interlude

| G | D | | Em7 | D/F# | G | | Em7 | D/F# | G | | :‖ |

| fear | myself. | ‖ | | | | | | | | |

2.

% Chorus

| G | | D | | Am | | | D/F# | | |
| fear | | myself. | ‖ I'm | off | the | deep | end. | Watch as | I | dive | in. | |

| G | | D | | Em7 | | Am | | |
| I'll | never | meet | the | | ground. | Crash through the | surface, | |

| D/F# | | G | D | Em7 | | Am | Am7 | |
| where they can't hurt | us. We're | far from the shallow | now. | | In the shal,-al | |

| D/F# | | G | D | Em7 | | Am | Am7 | |
| shal, -al - low, | | in the shal, shal, -al, | -al, -al - low. | | In the shal, -al | |

To Coda ⊕

| D/F# | | G | D | Em7 | | | ‖ |
| shal, -al - low, | we're | far from the shallow | now. | | | |

Bridge

| Bm | | D | | A | | Em7 | |
| Oh, | ah, | | | ah, | ah, | | oh, | |

D.S. al Coda   ⊕ **Coda**

| Bm | | D | | A | | Em7 | | ‖ |
| ah, | ah... | | | | ‖ | | | |

Skinny Love

Words and Music by Justin Vernon

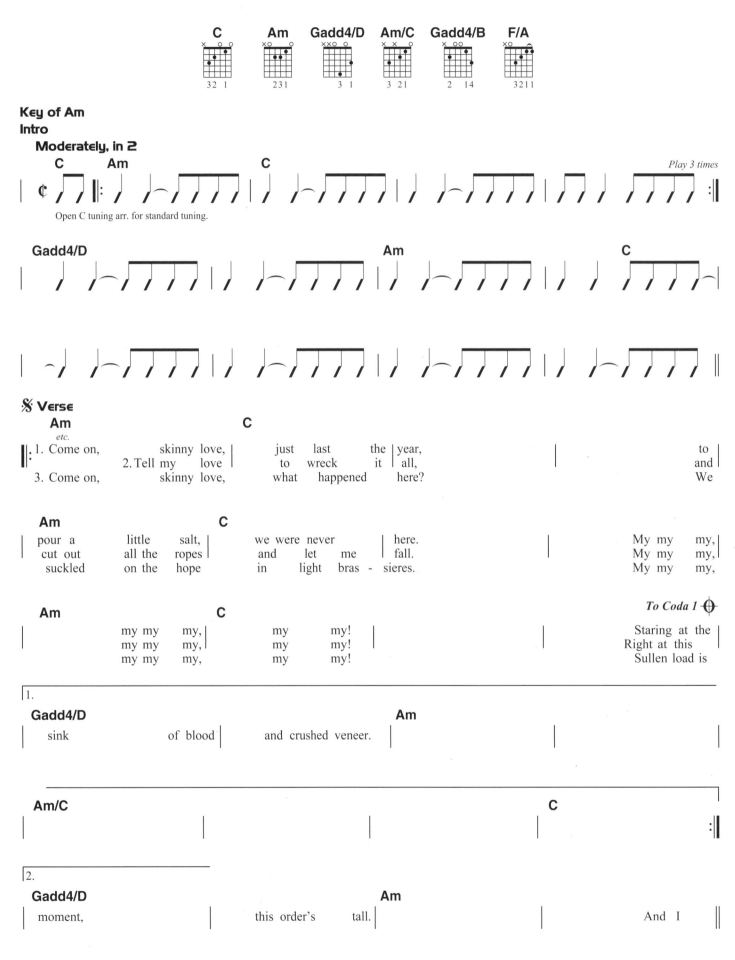

Key of Am
Intro
Moderately, in 2

Open C tuning arr. for standard tuning.

Verse

Am		**C**	
1. Come on,	skinny love,	just last the	year, to
2. Tell my love	to wreck it	all, and
3. Come on,	skinny love,	what happened here?	We

Am		**C**	
pour a little salt,	we were never	here.	My my my,
cut out all the ropes	and let me	fall.	My my my,
suckled on the hope	in light bras - sieres.		My my my,

		To Coda 1
Am	**C**	
my my my,	my my!	Staring at the
my my my,	my my!	Right at this
my my my,	my my!	Sullen load is

1.

Gadd4/D		**Am**
sink of blood	and crushed veneer.	

Am/C		**C**

2.

Gadd4/D	**Am**	
moment,	this order's tall.	And I

𝄋 𝄋 Bridge

C　　　　　　　　　　　　　　　　　　　　　　　　　　　　**Gadd4/B**　　　　　　　**F/A**

| told　you　to　be　pa | - tient,　　　and　I | told　you　to　be　fine. | 　　　　　And I |

C　　　　　　　　　　　　　　　　　　　　　　　　　　　　**Gadd4/B**　　　　　　　**F/A**

| told　you　to　be　bal | - anced,　　and　I | told　you　to　be　kind. | { And in the
{ And now |

C　　　　　　　　　　　　　　　　　　　　　　　　　　　　**Gadd4/B**　　　　　　　**F/A**

| morning　I'll　be　with | you,　　but it will | be　a　different　kind, | 　　and I'll be |
| all　your　love　is　wast | - ed,　　and then | who　the　hell　was　I? | 　　And I'm |

C　　　　　　　　　　　　　　　　　　　　　　　　　　　　**Gadd4/B**

| holding　all　the　tick | - ets　　and you'll be | owing　all　the　fines. |
| breaking　at　the　britch | - es,　　and　at　the | end　of　all　your　lines. |

F/A　　　　　　　　　　　　　　　　　　　*To Coda 2* ⊕　　　　　　　*D.S. al Coda 1*

| 　　　　| 　　　　| 　　　　| 　　　𝄇

⊕ **Coda 1**

Gadd4/D　　　　　　　　　　　　　　　　　　**Am**

| full,　　　so | slow　on　the split. | 　　　　　|

Am/C　　　　　　　　　　　　　*D.S.S. al Coda 2*　　　⊕ **Coda 2**

| 　　　| 　　　| 　　And I 𝄇 | 　　　𝄇

Outro

C　　　　　　　　　　　　　　**Gadd4/B**　　　　　　**F/A**　　　　**C**

| Who will | love　you? | Who will fight? | 　　　Who will |

Gadd4/B　　　　**F/A**

| fall | 　far　be - | hind? | 　　　|

　　　　　　　　　Am　　　　　　**C**　　　　　　　　　　　　　*Play 3 times*

| 𝄆 | 　　| 　　| 　　𝄇

Gadd4/D　　　　　　　　　　　**Am**　　　　　**Am/C**

| 　　| 　　| 　　𝄂

The Sound of Silence

Words and Music by Paul Simon

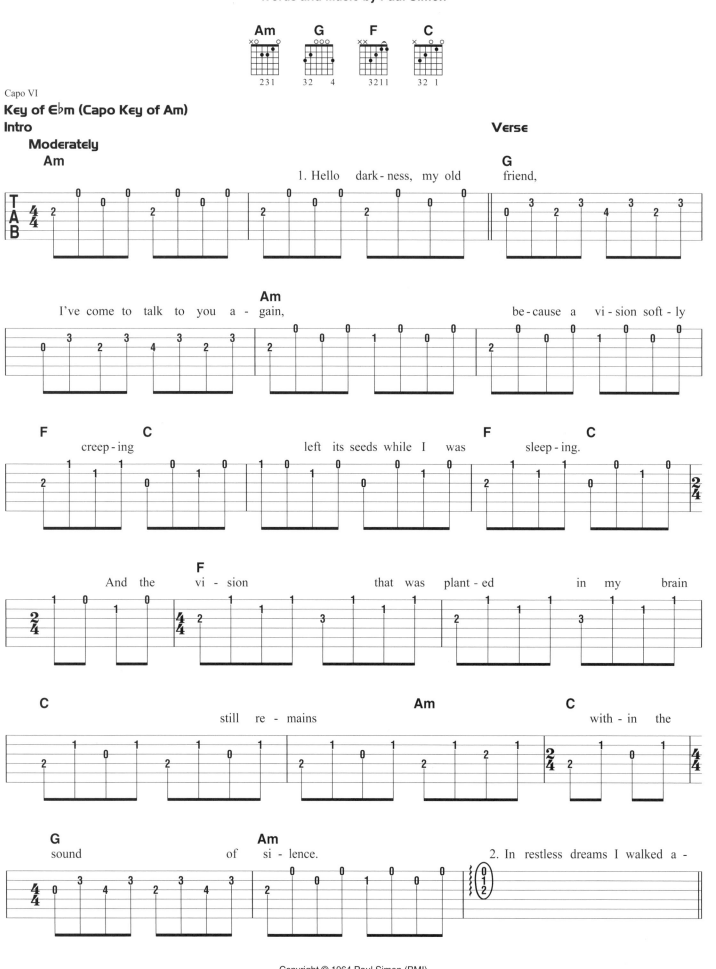

Verse

Strum

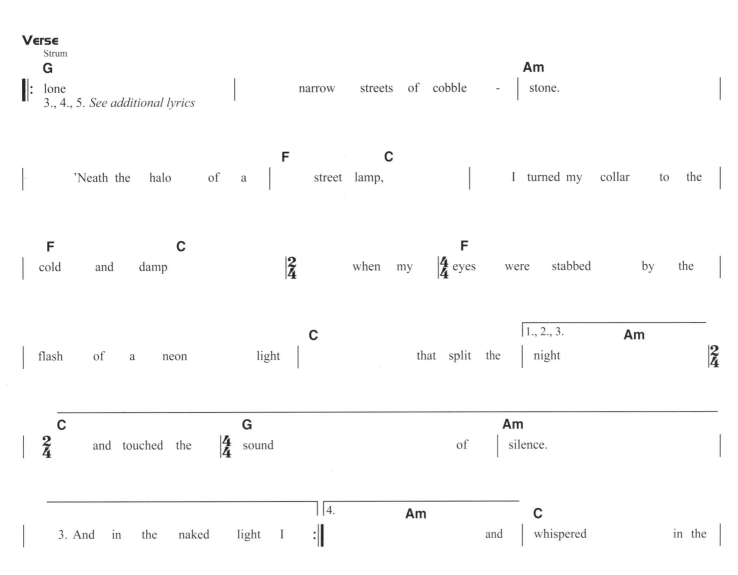

G ... Am
||: lone   narrow   streets   of   cobble - stone.
3., 4., 5. *See additional lyrics*

'Neath the halo of a | **F** street lamp, **C** | I turned my collar to the |

F cold and damp 2/4 when my 4/4 **F** eyes were stabbed by the |

flash of a neon **C** light | that split the |1., 2., 3. night **Am** 2/4

C 2/4 and touched the 4/4 **G** sound of | **Am** silence. |

3. And in the naked light I :|| |4. **Am** and | **C** whispered in the |

G sounds of **Am** silence."

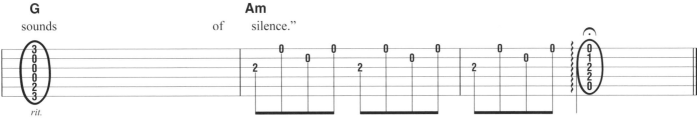

rit.

Additional Lyrics

3. And in the naked light I saw
Ten thousand people, maybe more.
People talking without speaking,
People hearing without list'ning.
People writing songs that voices never shared
And no one dared
Disturb the sound of silence.

4. "Fools," said I, "you do not know,
Silence like a cancer grows.
Hear my words that I might teach you.
Take my arms that I might reach you."
But my words like silent raindrops fell,
And echoed in the wells of silence.

5. And the people bowed and prayed
To the neon god they made.
And the sign flashed out its warning
In the words that it was forming.
And the sign said, "The words of the prophets are written on the subway walls
And tenement halls,
And whispered in the sounds of silence."

Southern Cross

Words and Music by Stephen Stills, Richard Curtis and Michael Curtis

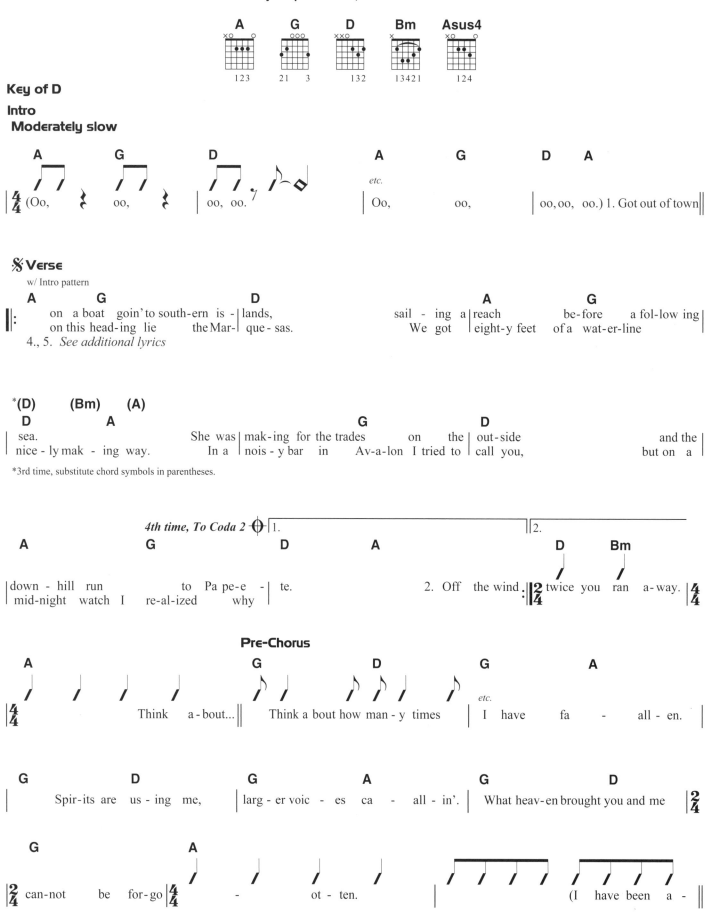

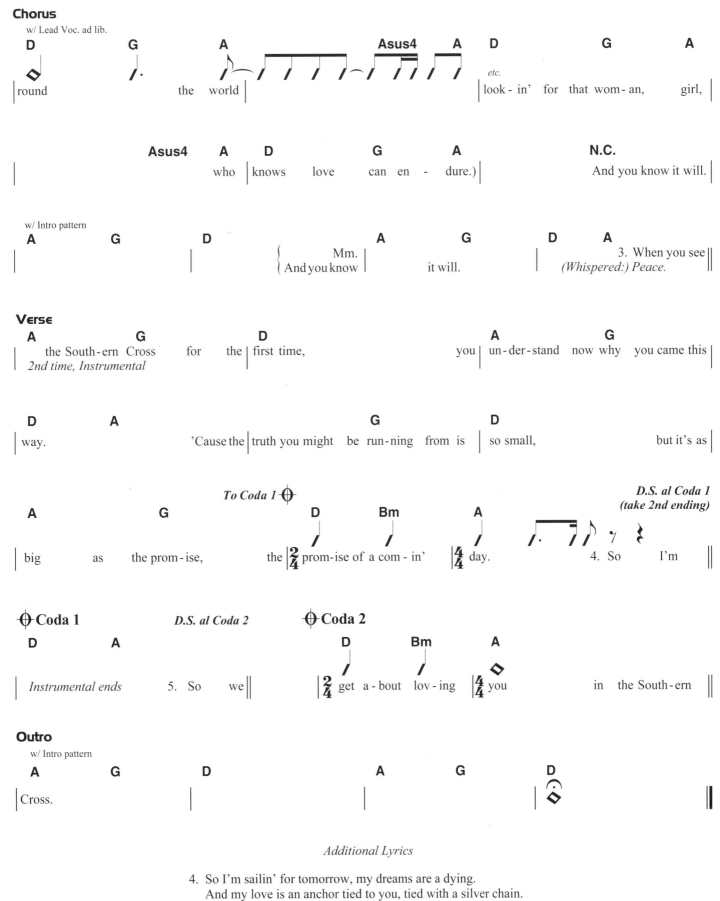

Additional Lyrics

4. So I'm sailin' for tomorrow, my dreams are a dying.
   And my love is an anchor tied to you, tied with a silver chain.
   I have my ship and all her flags are a flying.
   She is all that I have left and music is her name.

5. So we cheated and we lied and we tested.
   And we never failed to fail; it was the easiest thing to do.
   You will survive being bested.
   Somebody fine will come along, make me forget about loving you
   In the Southern Cross.

Sunny Came Home

Words and Music by Shawn Colvin and John Leventhal

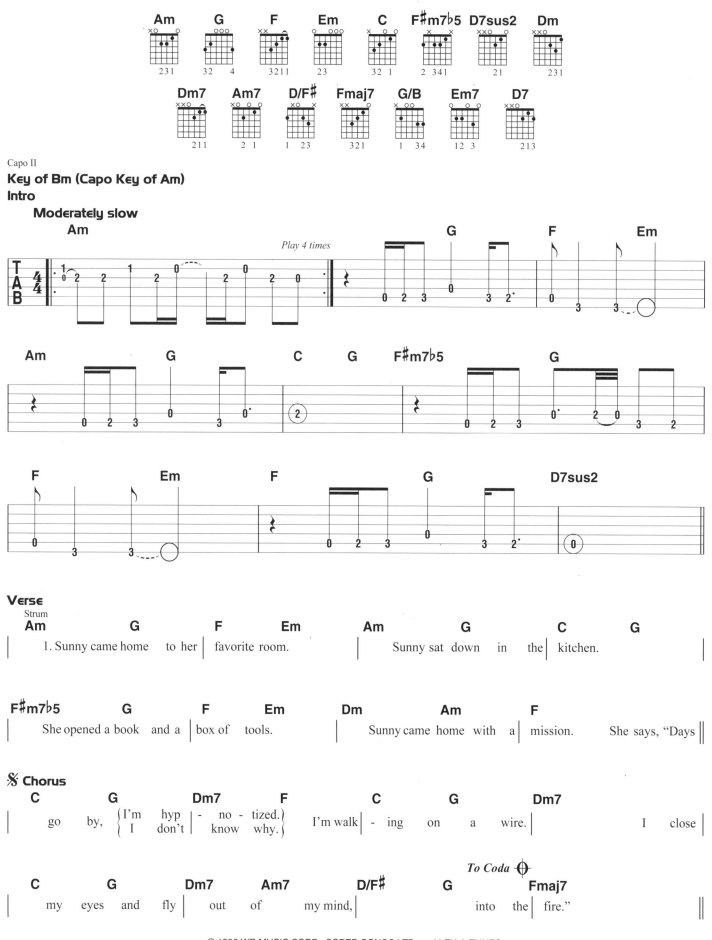

Capo II

Key of Bm (Capo Key of Am)

Intro

Moderately slow

Verse

Strum

| Am | G | F | Em | Am | G | C | G |
1. Sunny came home   to her   favorite room.   Sunny sat down   in   the   kitchen.

| F#m7♭5 | G | F | Em | Dm | Am | F |
She opened a book   and a   box of   tools.   Sunny came home   with a   mission.   She says, "Days

% Chorus

| C | G | Dm7 | F | C | G | Dm7 |
go   by,   {I'm   hyp - no - tized.} I'm walk - ing   on   a   wire.   I   close
{I   don't   know   why.}

To Coda ⊕

| C | G | Dm7 | Am7 | D/F# | G | Fmaj7 |
my   eyes   and   fly   out   of   my   mind,   into the   fire."

© 1996 WB MUSIC CORP., SCRED SONGS LTD. and LEV-A-TUNES
All Rights for SCRED SONGS LTD. Administered by WB MUSIC CORP.
All Rights for LEV-A-TUNES Administered by DOWNTOWN DLJ SONGS
All Rights Reserved   Used by Permission

Interlude

| Am   G | F   Em | Am   G | C   G   ‖

Verse

| Am   G   C   G | Am   G   C   Em |
| 2. Sunny came home with a | list of names. | She didn't believe in tran - | scendence. |

D.S. al Coda

| Fmaj7   G   Am   G/B | Dm7   Am   F |
| "Well, it's time for a few   small re- | pairs," she said. | Sunny came home with a | vengeance. She says, "Days ‖

⊕ Coda

| Fmaj7 |
| fire." |

Bridge

| G/B   Em7   Fmaj7 |
| Get ‖:   the   kids   and   bring | a   sweat - er.   Dry |
| the   years,   you   al | - ways   knew   it.   Strike |

	1.	2.
G/B Em7 Fmaj7		Fmaj7
is good and wind	is better.	Count :‖ and do it.
a match, go on		Oh, days ‖

Chorus

| C   G   Dm7   F | C   G   Dm7 |
| go   by, I'm hyp | - no - tized. I'm walk | - ing   on   a   wire. | I   close |

| C   G   Dm7   F | C   G   Dm7 |
| my   eyes and fly | out   of   my mind, | in - to   the   fire. | Oh,   light |

| C   G   Dm7   F | C   G   Dm7 |
| the   sky   and hold | on   tight. The world | is   burn - ing down. | She's   out |

| C   G   Dm7   Am7 | D/F♯   G   Fmaj7 |
| there on   her own | and she's   alright. | Sunny came | home. |

| D7   Am7 | D7   Am |
| | Sunny came | home.   ‖

89

Toes

Words and Music by Shawn Mullins, Zac Brown, Wyatt Durrette and John Driskell Hopkins

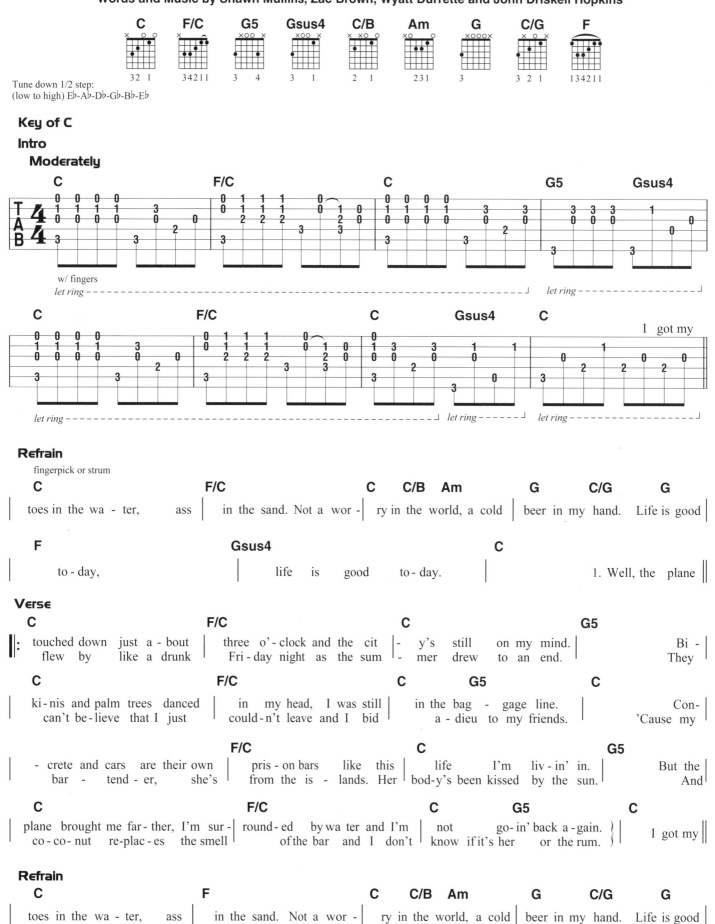

F		**G5**			**C**			**N.C.**	

| to - day, | life is good to - day. | A - di- os 'n' va - ya con ‖

Chorus
F   **C**

Di - os, { yeah, I'm leav - in' G A.
         { a long way from G A.
         { go - in' home, now, to stay.

G

And if it weren't | for te - qui - la and | pret - ty sen - or - i - tas, ah, |
Yes, and | all the mu - cha - chas, they | call me "Big Pa - pa" |
The sen - or - i - tas don't care - o when there's no di - ne - ro, yeah.

C   **N.C.**

I'd have no rea - son to | stay.) A - di - os 'n' va - ya con
when I throw pe - sos their | way. }
I got no mon - ey to | stay.)

3rd time, To Coda ⊕

F   **C**

Di - os, { yeah, I'm leav - in' G A.
         { a long way from G A.
         { go - in' home, now, to stay.

G   **N.C.**

Gon - na | lay in the hot sun and | roll a big fat one and, | and grab my gui - tar and ‖
Some - one | do me a fa - vor and | pour me some Jä - ger and | I'll grab my gui - tar and ‖

Interlude
w/ Intro pattern
                                        1.   2.   *D.S. al Coda*
C   **C**   **C**   **N.C.**

play. | **6** | 2. The four days :‖ | A - di os 'n' va - ya con ‖
play.

⊕ **Coda**
                    G5

Spoken: Just gon- na drive up | *by the lake* *and* put my ‖

Outro-Refrain
C   **F/C**   **C** **C/B Am**   **G**   **C/G**   **G**

ass in a lawn - chair, toes | in the clay. Not a wor | - ry in the world, a P. B. | R. on the way. Life is good ‖

F/C   **Gsus4**   **C**   **F** **G** **C**

to - day, | life is good to - day. | Rrr, ah! ‖

Touch of Grey

Words by Robert Hunter
Music by Jerry Garcia

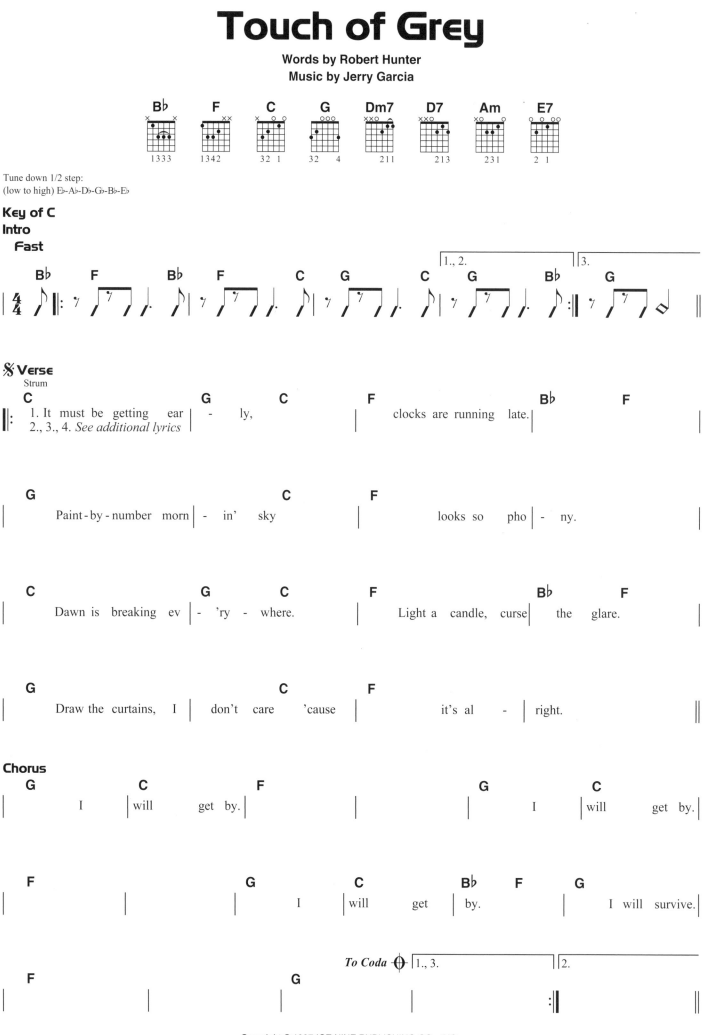

Tune down 1/2 step:
(low to high) Eb-Ab-Db-Gb-Bb-Eb

Key of C
Intro
Fast

Verse
Strum

1. It must be getting ear - ly, clocks are running late.
2., 3., 4. *See additional lyrics*

Paint - by - number morn - in' sky looks so pho - ny.

Dawn is breaking ev - 'ry - where. Light a candle, curse the glare.

Draw the curtains, I don't care 'cause it's al - right.

Chorus

I will get by. I will get by.

I will get by. I will survive.

To Coda

Bridge

Dm7		D7		G			
	It's a les- son		to me.			The

Dm7		D7		G		
deltas and the east		and the freeze.			

Am		E7		D7		G	
The A B C's			we all think	of		

D.S. al Coda
(take repeat)   **Coda**

C		F		G			
and try to win	a little love.					

Outro-Chorus

G		C		F			G		C	
We	will get by.				We	will get by.

F			G		C		Bb	F	G	
			We	will get	by.			We will survive.

Repeat and fade

F			G		

Additional Lyrics

2. I see you've got your list out; say your peace and get out.
Yes, I get the gist of it, but it's alright.
Sorry that you feel that way. The only thing there is to say:
Ev'ry silver lining's got a touch of grey.

3. I know the rent is in arrears, the dog has not been fed in years.
It's even worse than it appears, but it's alright.
Cows giving kerosene; kid can't read at seventeen.
The words he knows are all obscene, but it's alright.

4. The shoe is on the hand it fits, there's really nothing much to it.
Whistle through your teeth and spit 'cause it's alright.
Oh, well, a touch of grey, kinda suits you anyway.
That was all I had to say, and it's alright.

21 Guns

Words and Music by David Bowie, John Phillips, Billie Joe and Green Day

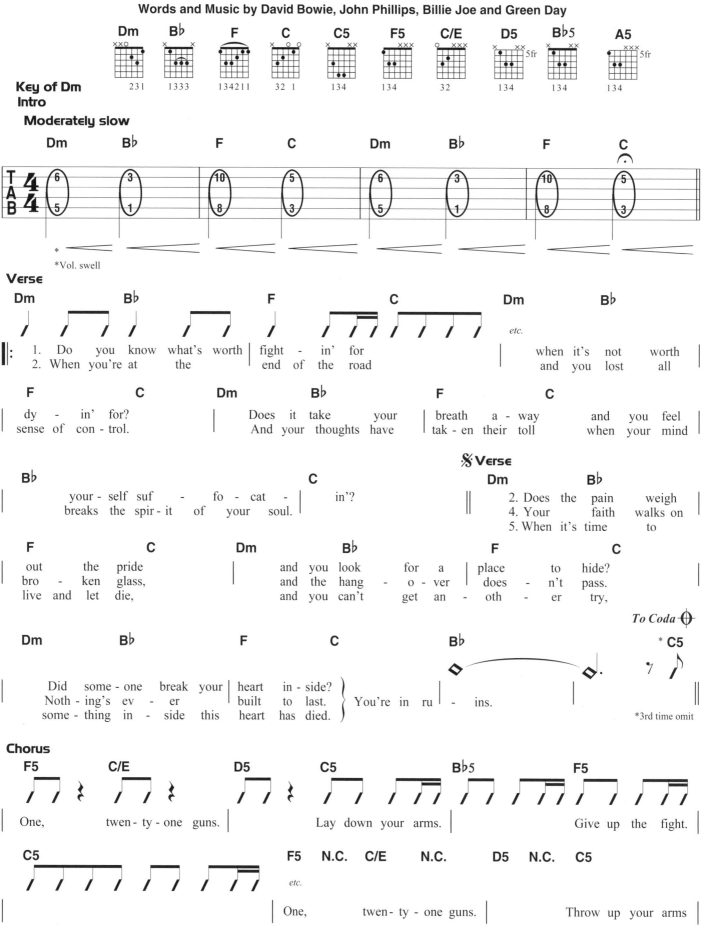

- contains samples of "All The Young Dudes" by David Bowie and "San Francisco (Be Sure To Wear Some Flowers In Your Hair)" by John Phillips

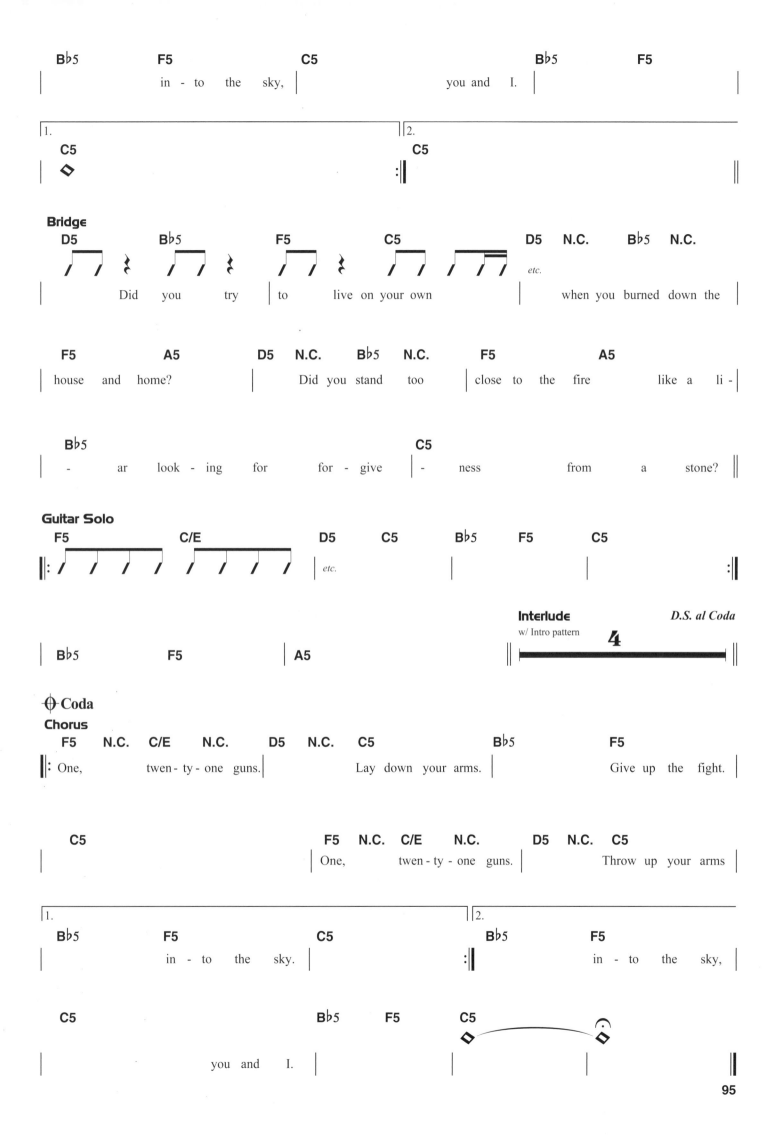

Upside Down

from the Universal Pictures and Imagine Entertainment film CURIOUS GEORGE
Words and Music by Jack Johnson

Intro (2 times)

|2.

8 :||

A   B

This   world   keeps   spin - nin'   and   there's

Bridge

G#m   F#m

no   time   to   waste.   Well,   it   all

D.S. al Coda

G#m   A   B

keeps | spin - nin',   spin - nin'   'round   and   'round   and

Gtr. 1: strum whole notes

E   F#m

Please   don't   go   a - way.

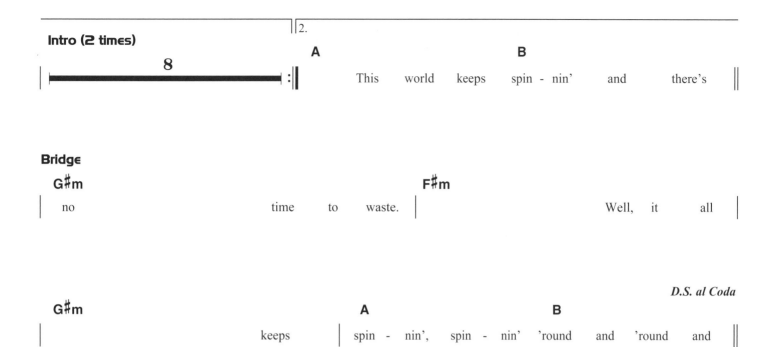

E   F#m

Please   don't   go   a - way.

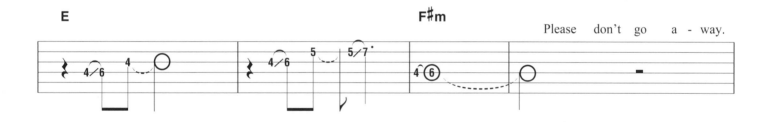

E   F#m

Is

Gtr. 1: arpeggiate chords

A   F#m   E   F#m   A   E

this   how   it's   sup - posed   to   be?   Is   this   how   it's   sup - posed   to   be?

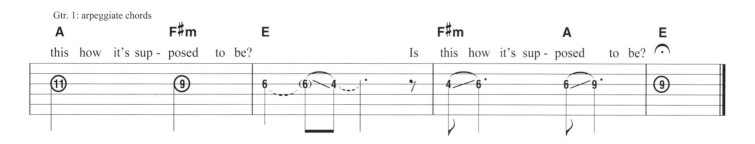

Wanted Dead or Alive

Words and Music by Jon Bon Jovi and Richie Sambora

D   Cadd9   G   F   C   D5

Key of D
Intro
Moderately slow

N.C.

*tie into beat one.

Play 3 times

1. It's

℅ Verse

D	Cadd9	G
all the same,	on - ly the names will change.	
times I sleep,	some - times it's not for days.	The
walk these streets, a load - ed six string on my back.		I

Cadd9	G	F	D
Ev - 'ry day it seems we're	wast - ing a - way.		An -
peo - ple I meet al - ways	go their sep - 'rate ways.		Some -
play for keeps, 'cause I	might not make it back.		I've been

		Cadd9	G
oth - er place, where the	fac - es are so cold,		I'd
times you tell the day by the	bot - tle that you drink.		And
ev - 'ry - where, still I'm	stand - ing tall,		I've

Cadd9	G	F	D
drive all night just to	get back home.		I'm a
times when you're a - lone	all you do is think.		
seen a mil - lion fac - es, and I've	rocked them all.		

Chorus

C	G	F	D
cow - boy, on a	steel horse I ride.		I'm

To Coda ⊕

C	G	C	D	F	D
want - ed, * (Want - ed.)		dead or a - live.			

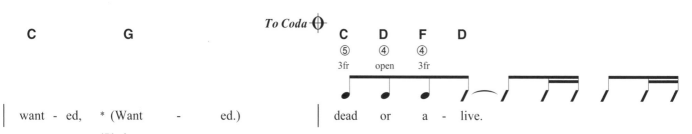

*Bkgds. sung 2nd & 3rd times only.

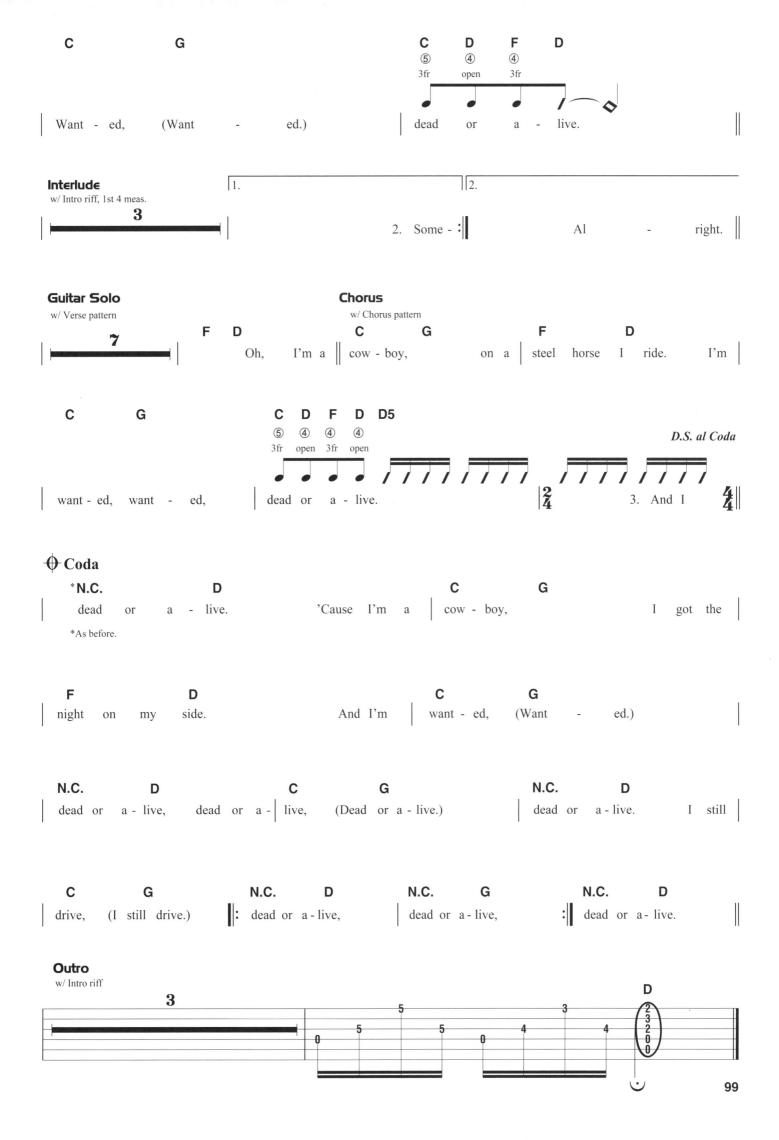

C   G   C   D   F   D

Want - ed,   (Want - ed.)   dead   or   a - live.

Interlude
w/ Intro riff, 1st 4 meas.

1.   2.

3   2. Some - :‖   Al - right. ‖

Guitar Solo
w/ Verse pattern   **Chorus**
w/ Chorus pattern

7   F   D   C   G   F   D

Oh,   I'm a ‖ cow - boy,   on a | steel horse I ride.   I'm

C   G   C   D   F   D   D5

D.S. al Coda

want - ed,   want - ed,   dead or a - live.   2/4   3. And I   4/4‖

⊕ Coda

*N.C.   D   C   G

dead   or   a - live.   'Cause I'm a | cow - boy,   I   got the |
*As before.

F   D   C   G

night   on   my   side.   And I'm | want - ed,   (Want - ed.) |

N.C.   D   C   G   N.C.   D

dead or a - live,   dead or a - | live,   (Dead or a - live.)   dead or a - live.   I still |

C   G   N.C.   D   N.C.   G   N.C.   D

drive,   (I still drive.)   ‖: dead or a - live, | dead or a - live,   :‖ dead or a - live.   ‖

Outro
w/ Intro riff

99

The Weight

By J.R. Robertson

Key of A
Intro
   Slow, in 2
      N.C.

§ **Verse**
   Strum

A   **C#m**   **D**
1. I pulled   into   Naz -areth,   was   feeling 'bout   half   past
2. - 5. *See additional lyrics*

A   **C#m**
dead.   I just   need   some place   where

D   **A**
I can lay   my   head.   "Hey,   mister,   can you

C#m   **D**   **A**
tell   me   where   a man might find   a bed?"

                    C#m   **D**   **A**
He just grinned   and shook   my   hand;   "No," was all   he said.

Chorus

| A | E | D | | A | E |

Take a load off, | Fanny. Take a load for |

| D | | A | E | D |

free. | Take a load off, | Fanny. |

| | And | | you | put the load right on | **2/4** me. | **¢** ||

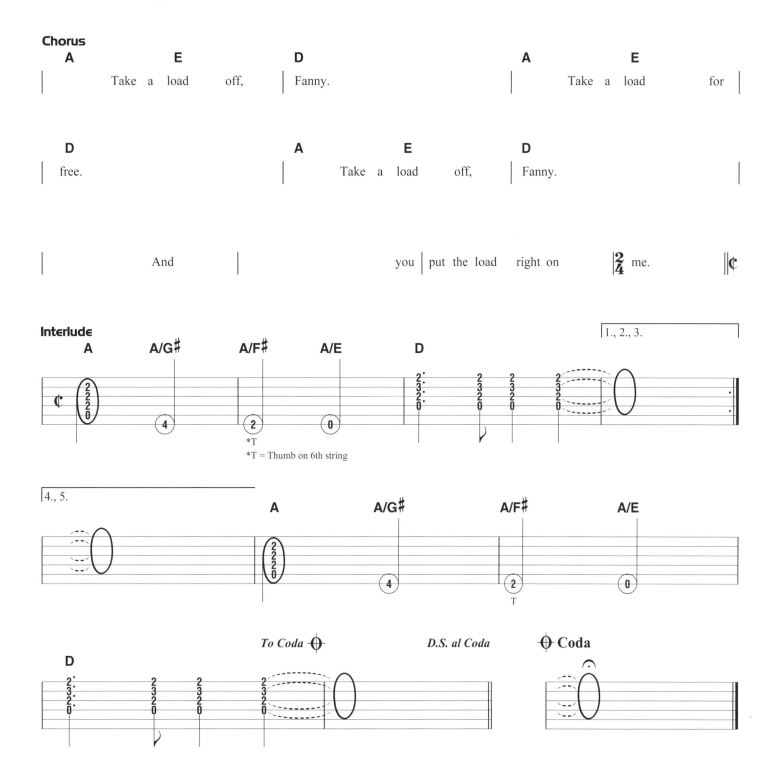

*T = Thumb on 6th string

Additional Lyrics

2. I picked up my bag; I went looking for a place to hide,
When I saw Carmen and the devil walking side by side.
I said, "Hey, Carmen, come on, let's go downtown."
She said, "I gotta go, but my friend can stick around."

3. Go down, Miss Moses, there's nothing you can say.
It's just ol' Luke, and Luke's waiting on the judgment day.
"Well, Luke, my friend, what about young Anna Lee?"
He said, "Do me a favor, son; won't you stay and keep Anna Lee company?"

4. Crazy Chester followed me and he caught me in the fog.
He said, "I will fix your rack if you'll take Jack, my dog."
I said, "Wait a minute, Chester, you know I'm a peaceful man."
He said, "That's okay, boy; won't you feed him when you can?"

5. Catch a cannonball now, to take me down the line.
My bag is sinking low, and I do believe it's time
To get back to Miss Fanny. You know she's the only one
Who sent me here with her regards for everyone.

White Horse

Words and Music by Taylor Swift and Liz Rose

C5   Fsus2   Am7   Gsus4   G   C   Fadd9   G/B   B♭

Key of C
Intro
Moderately

C5   Fsus2   Am7   Fsus2

w/ pick & fingers
let ring throughout

Verse

C5
1. Say you're sorry,   that face   of an angel   comes out
2. Maybe I was naive,   got lost in your   eyes and   Fsus2

Am7   Fsus2   C5
just when you need it to   as I paced back and forth
never really had a chance.   My mistake, I didn't know

Fsus2   Am7   Fsus2
all this time 'cause I   honestly believed in   you.   Hold-
to be in love you had to   fight to have the upper hand.   I had

Am7   Fsus2
- ing on, the days   drag on.   Stupid girl,
so many dreams about   you and me;   happy

Gsus4   *G
I should've known, I should've known   that I'm not a prin -
endings,   now I know
*Let chord ring

Chorus

C   Am7   Fadd9
- cess, this ain't a fair-y tale. I'm not the one   you'll sweep off her feet, lead

Gsus4   G   C   Am7
her up the stairwell. This ain't   Hollywood, this is a small   town. I was a dream-

Fadd9			**Gsus4**	**G**		**Am7**	**G/B**
- er before you went and let	me down.	Now it's too		late for you	and your white

|1.   **|2.**

Fadd9		**C5**			**Fadd9**	
horse to come a -	round.			:‖ horse	to come a - ‖

Guitar Solo

C	**Am7**	**Fadd9**	**Gsus4**	**G**
round.				‖

Bridge

Am7	**G/B**	**Fadd9**		**C**	**G/B**
And there you are on your	knees,			beggin' for forgiveness,	

Fadd9		**C**	**G/B**	**Fadd9**	
beggin' for me,		just like I always wanted,	but I'm so	sor -

B♭		*__**B♭**__		**Chorus** **C**	
- ry.		'Cause I'm not your prin	‖ - cess,	this ain't a fair -

*Let chord ring

Am7		**Fadd9**		**Gsus4**	**G**
y tale. I'm gonna find	someone someday who might	actually treat me well. This is a

C		**Am7**	**Fadd9**	
big world, that was a small	town there in my rear	view mirror disappear -

Gsus4	**G**	**Am7**	**G/B**	**Fadd9**	
in' now. And it's too	late for you and your white	horse, now it's too

Am7	**G/B**	**Fadd9**	**Outro** **C5**	
late for you and your white	horse to catch me	‖ now.	

Fsus2	**Am7**	**Fsus2**	**C5**	
Oh,		try and catch me now,	oh.

Fsus2	**Am7**	**Fadd9**	**C**	
It's too late	to catch me	now.	‖

You Were Meant for Me

Words and Music by Jewel Murray and Steve Poltz

Cadd9   G6/B   C   E   D   G   G5/F#   Am7   Bm   C/B   Bm/F#

Tune down 1/2 step:
(low to high) Eb-Ab-Db-Gb-Bb-Eb

Key of G
Intro
Moderately

Cadd9   G6/B   C   Em

*3rd time, **A Tempo**.

Verse
w/ Intro pattern simile

Cadd9   **G6/B**
1. I hear the clock,   it's   six A.   M.
2. I called my mom - ma, she was   out for a walk.   Con -
3. I brush my teeth, I put the   cap back on.

C   **Em**
soled a cup of cof - fee but it   where I've been.
    I know you hate it when I   did - n't wan - na talk. So I
          leave the light on. I

Cadd9   **G6/B**
   I got my eggs, I got my   pan - cakes too.   I
picked up the pa - per, it was   more bad news;   more
pick a book up and then I   turn the sheets down   and then I

C   **D**
got my ma - ple syr - up, ev - 'ry -   thing but you.
hearts be - ing bro - ken or   peo - ple be - ing used.
take a deep breath and a   good look a - round.

Cadd9   **G6/B**
   I break the yolks and make a   smile - y face.
Put on my coat in the pour   - ing rain.
Put on my P J's and   hop in - to bed. I'm

C   **Em**
   I kind - a like it in my   brand - new place. Wipe the
   I saw a mov - ie, it just   was - n't the same 'cause I
half a - live but I feel   most - ly dead. I, I

Cadd9 .... **G6/B**

spots off of the mirr'r, don't leave my	keys in the door.	I
it was hap - py, oh,	I was sad, and	
try and tell my - self it - 'll all	be al - right.	

C .... **D**

| nev - er put wet tow - els | on the | floor an - y - more |
| it made me miss you, | oh, so bad |
| I just should - n't think | an - y - more to - night, | 'cause

Chorus

C .... **D** .... **G** .. **G5/F#** .... **Em**

| dreams last | so long | e - ven af - ter you're gone. | |

C .... **D** .... **G** .. **G5/F#** .... **Em**

| I know that | you love me and | soon you will see | you were |

To Coda ⊕ |1.

C .... **D** .... **Em**

| meant for me and | I was meant for | you. | :‖

|2.

Bridge

Am7 .... **D**

| I ‖ go a - bout my bus - 'ness, I'm | do - ing fine. Be - sides, a | *etc.*

Bm .... **D** .... **C** .. **C/B** .. **Am7**

| what would I say if I had | you on the line? | Same old sto - ry, not |

D.S. al Coda
(take repeat)

D .... **Bm/F#** .... **Em**

| much to say. | Hearts are bro - ken ev - 'ry | day. | ‖
 .... *rit.* ....

⊕ **Coda**

Outro

.... **C** .... **D** **Cadd9**

| Yeah, you were ‖ meant for me and | I was meant for | you. | |

G6/B .... **C** .... **Em**

| | | | ‖
 .... *rit.*

105

New Kid in Town

Words and Music by John David Souther, Don Henley and Glenn Frey

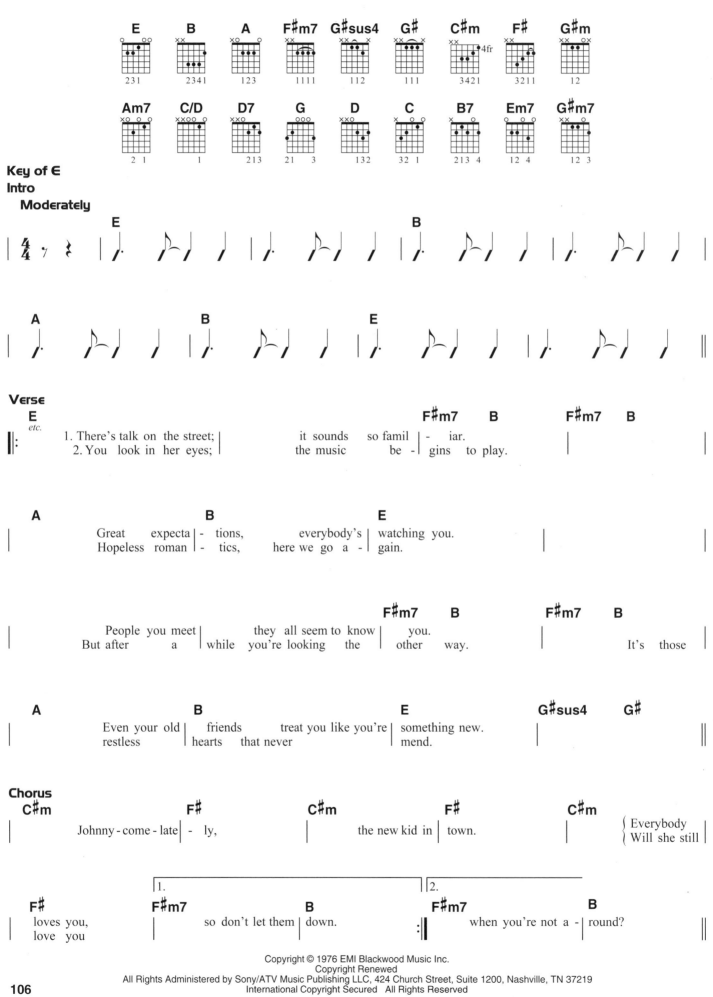

Guitar Solo

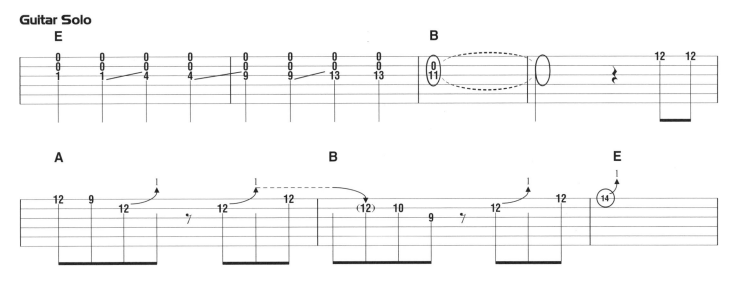

Bridge

There's so man - y   things   you should have

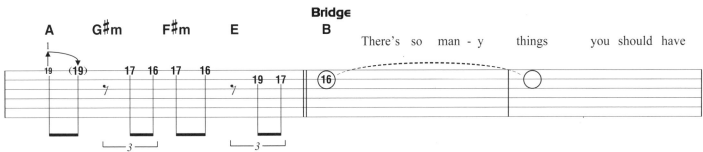

E

| told   her, | | | but night after | night   you're willing to |

B

C#m   F#   Am7   C/D   D7

| hold   her,   just | hold   her. | Tears   on   your | shoulder. ‖

Verse

G   Am7   D   Am7   D

| 3. There's talk on the | street;   it's there   to re - | mind   you | |

C   D   G

| that it doesn't really | matter   which side | you're on. | |

                                                                    Am7   D   Am7   D

| You're walking away | and they're talking be - | hind   you. | They will |

C   D   G   B7

| never   forget   you till | somebody new comes a - | long. | ‖

107

Chorus

Em7		A		Em7		A	
	Where you been	lately?			There's a new kid	in	town.

Em7		A		Am7		B	
	Everybody	loves him, don't they?			Now he's holding	her, and you're still a-

Outro

E		G#m7		A		B	
	round.		Oh, my,	my.		There's a new kid in

E		G#m7		A		B	
	town,					just another new kid in

E		G#m7		A		Am7	
	town.					

E			C#m		
	Ooh, hoo.	Everybody's talking 'bout the	new kid in town.	

E			C#m		
	Ooh, hoo.	Everybody's walking like the	new kid in town.	There's a

E			C#m		
	new kid in town.	I don't want to hear it. There's a	new kid in town. I	don't want to hear it. There's a

Repeat and fade

E			C#m		
new kid in town.		There's a	new kid in town.	There's a

RHYTHM TAB LEGEND

Rhythm Tab is a form of notation that adds rhythmic values to the traditional tab staff.

TABLATURE graphically represents the guitar fingerboard. Each horizontal line represents a string, and each number represents a fret. Rhythmic values are shown using ovals, stems, and dots.

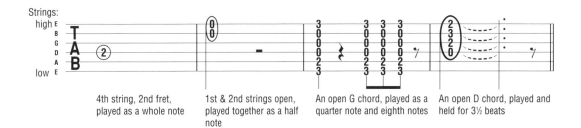

4th string, 2nd fret, played as a whole note

1st & 2nd strings open, played together as a half note

An open G chord, played as a quarter note and eighth notes

An open D chord, played and held for 3½ beats

Definitions for Special Guitar Notation

HALF-STEP BEND: Strike the note and bend up 1/2 step.

WHOLE-STEP BEND: Strike the note and bend up one step.

SLIGHT (MICROTONE) BEND: Strike the note and bend up 1/4 step.

BEND AND RELEASE: Strike the note and bend up as indicated, then release back to the original note. Only the first note is struck.

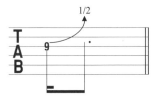
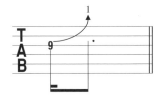
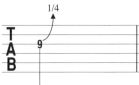
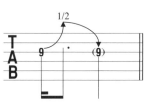

PRE-BEND: Bend the note as indicated, then strike it.

GRACE NOTE PRE-BEND AND RELEASE: Bend the note as indicated. Strike it and release the bend back to the original note.

UNISON BEND: Strike the two notes simultaneously and bend the lower note up to the pitch of the higher.

HOLD BEND: While sustaining bent note, strike note on different string.

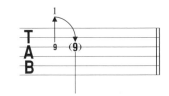

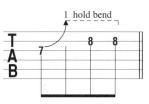

VIBRATO: The string is vibrated by rapidly bending and releasing the note with the fretting hand.

WIDE VIBRATO: The pitch is varied to a greater degree by vibrating with the fretting hand.

HAMMER-ON: Strike the first (lower) note with one finger, then sound the higher note (on the same string) with another finger by fretting it without picking.

PULL-OFF: Place both fingers on the notes to be sounded. Strike the first note and without picking, pull the finger off to sound the second (lower) note.

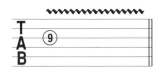
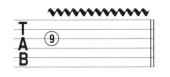
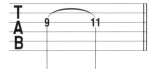
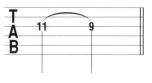

HAMMER FROM NOWHERE: Sound note(s) by hammering with fret hand finger only.

GRACE NOTE SLUR: Strike the note and immediately hammer-on (or pull-off) as indicated.

GRACE NOTE SLUR (CLUSTER): Strike the notes and immediately hammer-on (or pull-off) as indicated.

LEGATO SLIDE: Strike the first note and then slide the same fret-hand finger up or down to the second note. The second note is not struck.

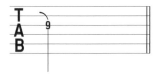

SHIFT SLIDE: Same as legato slide, except the second note is struck.

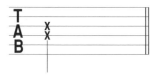

GRACE NOTE SLIDE: Quickly slide into the note from below or above.

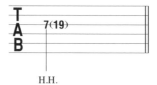

TRILL: Very rapidly alternate between the notes indicated by continuously hammering on and pulling off.

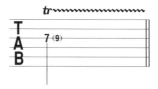

TAPPING: Hammer ("tap") the fret indicated with the pick-hand index or middle finger and pull off to the note fretted by the fret hand.

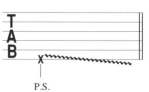

NATURAL HARMONIC: Strike the note while the fret-hand lightly touches the string directly over the fret indicated.

Harm.

PINCH HARMONIC: The note is fretted normally and a harmonic is produced by adding the edge of the thumb or the tip of the index finger of the pick hand to the normal pick attack.

P.H.

HARP HARMONIC: The note is fretted normally and a harmonic is produced by gently resting the pick hand's index finger directly above the indicated fret (in parentheses) while the pick hand's thumb or pick assists by plucking the appropriate string.

H.H.

PICK SCRAPE: The edge of the pick is rubbed down (or up) the string, producing a scratchy sound.

P.S.

MUFFLED STRINGS: A percussive sound is produced by laying the fret hand across the string(s) without depressing, and striking them with the pick hand.

PALM MUTING: The note is partially muted by the pick hand lightly touching the string(s) just before the bridge.

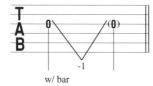

P.M. - - - - - - - - - ⌐

RAKE: Drag the pick across the strings indicated with a single motion.

rake - ⌐

TREMOLO PICKING: The note is picked as rapidly and continuously as possible.

ARPEGGIATE: Play the notes of the chord indicated by quickly rolling them from bottom to top.

VIBRATO BAR DIVE AND RETURN: The pitch of the note or chord is dropped a specified number of steps (in rhythm), then returned to the original pitch.

w/ bar

VIBRATO BAR SCOOP: Depress the bar just before striking the note, then quickly release the bar.

w/ bar - - - - - - - - ⌐

VIBRATO BAR DIP: Strike the note and then immediately drop a specified number of steps, then release back to the original pitch.

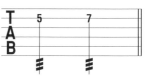

w/ bar - - - - - - - ⌐

Additional Musical Definitions

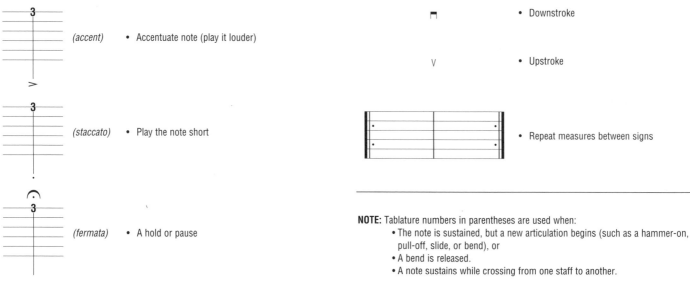

NOTE: Tablature numbers in parentheses are used when:
- The note is sustained, but a new articulation begins (such as a hammer-on, pull-off, slide, or bend), or
- A bend is released.
- A note sustains while crossing from one staff to another.

Guitar Chord Songbooks

Each 6" x 9" book includes complete lyrics, chord symbols, and guitar chord diagrams.

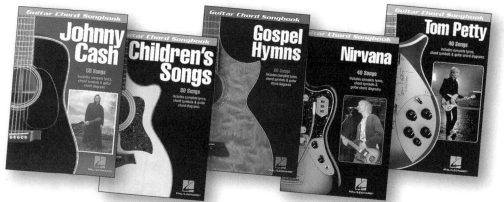

Acoustic Hits
00701787 . . . . $14.99

Acoustic Rock
00699540 . . . . $22.99

Alabama
00699914 . . . . $14.95

The Beach Boys
00699566 . . . . $19.99

Bluegrass
00702585 . . . . $14.99

Johnny Cash
00699648 . . . . $19.99

Children's Songs
00699539 . . . . $17.99

Christmas Carols
00699536 . . . . $14.99

Christmas Songs
00119911 . . . . $14.99

Eric Clapton
00699567 . . . . $19.99

Classic Rock
00699598 . . . . $20.99

Coffeehouse Hits
00703318 . . . . $14.99

Country
00699534 . . . . $17.99

Country Favorites
00700609 . . . . $14.99

Country Hits
00140859 . . . . $14.99

Country Standards
00700608 . . . . $12.95

Cowboy Songs
00699636 . . . . $19.99

Creedence Clearwater Revival
00701786 . . . . $16.99

Jim Croce
00148087 . . . . $14.99

Crosby, Stills & Nash
00701609 . . . . $17.99

John Denver
02501697 . . . . $19.99

Neil Diamond
00700606 . . . . $22.99

Disney – 2nd Edition
00295786 . . . . $19.99

The Doors
00699888 . . . . $22.99

Eagles
00122917 . . . . $19.99

Early Rock
00699916 . . . . $14.99

Folksongs
00699541 . . . . $16.99

Folk Pop Rock
00699651 . . . . $17.99

40 Easy Strumming Songs
00115972 . . . . $16.99

Four Chord Songs
00701611 . . . . $16.99

Glee
00702501 . . . . $14.99

Gospel Hymns
00700463 . . . . $16.99

Grateful Dead
00139461 . . . . $17.99

Green Day
00103074 . . . . $17.99

Irish Songs
00701044 . . . . $16.99

Michael Jackson
00137847 . . . . $14.99

Billy Joel
00699632 . . . . $22.99

Elton John
00699732 . . . . $17.99

Ray LaMontagne
00130337 . . . . $12.99

Latin Songs
00700973 . . . . $14.99

Love Songs
00701043 . . . . $14.99

Bob Marley
00701704 . . . . $17.99

Bruno Mars
00125332 . . . . $12.99

Paul McCartney
00385035 . . . . $19.99

Steve Miller
00701146 . . . . $12.99

Modern Worship
00701801 . . . . $19.99

Motown
00699734 . . . . $19.99

Willie Nelson
00148273 . . . . $17.99

Nirvana
00699762 . . . . $17.99

Roy Orbison
00699752 . . . . $19.99

Peter, Paul & Mary
00103013 . . . . $19.99

Tom Petty
00699883 . . . . $17.99

Pink Floyd
00139116 . . . . $17.99

Pop/Rock
00699538 . . . . $19.99

Praise & Worship
00699634 . . . . $14.99

Elvis Presley
00699633 . . . . $17.99

Queen
00702395 . . . . $17.99

Red Hot Chili Peppers
00699710 . . . . $24.99

The Rolling Stones
00137716 . . . . $19.99

Bob Seger
00701147 . . . . $16.99

Carly Simon
00121011 . . . . $14.99

Sting
00699921 . . . . $24.99

Three Chord Acoustic Songs
00123860 . . . . $16.99

Three Chord Songs
00699720 . . . . $17.99

Two-Chord Songs
00119236 . . . . $16.99

U2
00137744 . . . . $19.99

Hank Williams
00700607 . . . . $16.99

Stevie Wonder
00120862 . . . . $14.99

Prices and availability subject to change without notice.

HAL•LEONARD®
Visit Hal Leonard online at **www.halleonard.com**

STRUM & SING

The Strum & Sing series for guitar and ukulele provides an unplugged and pared-down approach to your favorite songs — just the chords and the lyrics, with nothing fancy. These easy-to-play arrangements are designed for both aspiring and professional musicians.

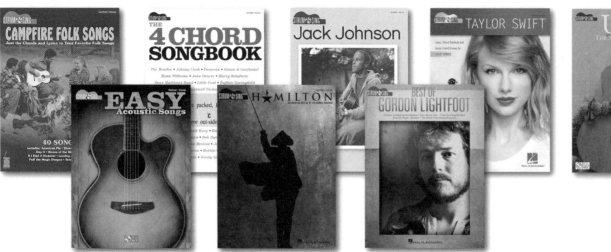

GUITAR

Acoustic Classics
00191891 ....$15.99

Adele
00159855 ....$12.99

Sara Bareilles
00102354 ....$12.99

The Beatles
00172234 ....$17.99

Blues
00159335 ....$12.99

Zac Brown Band
02501620 ....$19.99

Colbie Caillat
02501725 ....$14.99

Campfire Folk Songs
02500686 ....$15.99

Chart Hits of 2014-2015
00142554 ....$12.99

Chart Hits of 2015-2016
00156248 ....$12.99

Best of Kenny Chesney
00142457 ....$14.99

Christmas Carols
00348351 ....$14.99

Christmas Songs
00171332 ....$14.99

Kelly Clarkson
00146384 ....$14.99

Coffeehouse Songs for Guitar
00285991 ....$14.99

Leonard Cohen
00265489 ....$14.99

Dear Evan Hansen
00295108 ....$16.99

John Denver Collection
02500632 ....$17.99

Disney
00233900 ....$17.99

Eagles
00157994 ....$14.99

Easy Acoustic Songs
00125478 ....$19.99

Billie Eilish
00363094 ....$14.99

The Five-Chord Songbook
02501718 ....$14.99

Folk Rock Favorites
02501669 ....$14.99

Folk Songs
02501482 ....$14.99

The Four-Chord Country Songbook
00114936 ....$15.99

The Four Chord Songbook
02501533 ....$14.99

Four Chord Songs
00249581 ....$16.99

The Greatest Showman
00278383 ....$14.99

Hamilton
00217116 ....$15.99

Jack Johnson
02500858 ....$19.99

Robert Johnson
00191890 ....$12.99

Carole King
00115243 ....$10.99

Best of Gordon Lightfoot
00139393 ....$15.99

Dave Matthews Band
02501078 ....$10.95

John Mayer
02501636 ....$19.99

The Most Requested Songs
02501748 ....$16.99

Jason Mraz
02501452 ....$14.99

**Tom Petty –
Wildflowers & All the Rest**
00362682 ....$14.99

Elvis Presley
00198890 ....$12.99

Queen
00218578 ....$12.99

Rock Around the Clock
00103625 ....$12.99

Rock Ballads
02500872 ....$9.95

Rocketman
00300469 ....$17.99

Ed Sheeran
00152016 ....$14.99

The Six-Chord Songbook
02502277 ....$17.99

Chris Stapleton
00362625 ....$19.99

Cat Stevens
00116827 ....$17.99

Taylor Swift
00159856 ....$14.99

The Three-Chord Songbook
00211634 ....$12.99

Top Christian Hits
00156331 ....$12.99

Top Hits of 2016
00194288 ....$12.99

Keith Urban
00118558 ....$14.99

The Who
00103667 ....$12.99

Yesterday
00301629 ....$14.99

Neil Young – Greatest Hits
00138270 ....$15.99

UKULELE

The Beatles
00233899 ....$16.99

Colbie Caillat
02501731 ....$10.99

Coffeehouse Songs
00138238 ....$14.99

John Denver
02501694 ....$17.99

The 4-Chord Ukulele Songbook
00114331 ....$16.99

Jack Johnson
02501702 ....$19.99

John Mayer
02501706 ....$10.99

The Most Requested Songs
02501453 ....$15.99

Jason Mraz
02501753 ....$14.99

Pop Songs for Kids
00284415 ....$16.99

Sing-Along Songs
02501710 ....$16.99

HAL•LEONARD®

halleonard.com
Visit our website to see full song lists
or order from your favorite retailer.

*Prices, contents and availability
subject to change without notice.*